# Health Essentials

## Self-Hypnosis

**Elaine Sheehan** is qualified in Applied Psychology and clini-
cally trained in both Hypnotherapy and Psychotherapy. In
addition to running a busy private practice in Leeds, she works
for major corporate bodies and community and mental health
services and she is currently designing her own courses for use
in these fields. In the past she has worked as a lecturer and
trainer of therapists with British Hypnosis Research, running
courses and workshops in hospitals across the UK.

# The Health Essentials Series

There is a growing number of people who find themselves attracted to holistic or alternative therapies and natural approaches to maintaining optimum health and vitality. The *Health Essentials* series is designed to help the newcomer by presenting high quality introductions to all the main complementary health subjects. Each book presents all the essential information on each therapy, explaining what it is, how it works and what it can do for the reader. Advice is also given, where possible, on how to begin using the therapy at home, together with comprehensive lists of courses and classes available worldwide.

The *Health Essentials* titles are all written by practising experts in their fields. Exceptionally clear and concise, each text is supported by attractive illustrations.

Series Medical Consultant
Dr John Cosh MD, FRCP

*In the same series*

*Acupuncture* by Peter Mole
*Alexander Technique* by Richard Brennan
*Aromatherapy* by Christine Wildwood
*Ayurveda* by Scott Gerson
*Chi Kung* by James MacRitchie
*Chinese Medicine* by Tom Williams
*Colour Therapy* by Pauline Wills
*Flower Remedies* by Christine Wildwood
*Herbal Medicine* by Vicki Pitman
*Kinesiology* by Ann Holdway
*Massage* by Stewart Mitchell
*Reflexology* by Inge Dougans with Suzanne Ellis
*Shiatsu* by Elaine Liechti
*Skin and Body Care* by Sidra Shaukat
*Spiritual Healing* by Jack Angelo
*Vitamin Guide* by Hasnain Walji

Health Essentials

# SELF-HYPNOSIS

## Effective Techniques
## for Everyday Problems

ELAINE SHEEHAN

ELEMENT
Shaftesbury, Dorset ● Rockport, Massachusetts
Brisbane, Queensland

© Elaine Sheehan 1995

First published in Great Britain in 1995 by
Element Books Limited
Shaftesbury, Dorset

Published in the USA in 1995 by
Element, Inc.
42 Broadway, Rockport, MA 01966

Published in Australia in 1995 by
Element Books Limited
for Jacaranda Wiley Limited
33 Park Road, Milton, Brisbane 4064

Cover design by Max Fairbrother
Design by Roger Lightfoot
Typeset by The Electronic Book Factory Ltd, Fife
Printed and bound in Great Britain by
Biddles Ltd, Guildford & King's Lynn.

British Library Cataloguing in Publication
data available

Library of Congress Cataloging in Publication
data available

ISBN 1–85230–639–4

*Note from the Publisher*

Any information given in any book in the *Health Essentials* series is
not intended to be taken as a replacement for medical advice. Any
person with a condition requiring medical attention should consult
a qualified medical practitioner or suitable therapist.

In memory of my dear mother
who showed inspiring love,
courage and strength

# Acknowledgements

I AM GRATEFUL to my teachers and particularly my patients and students who continue to be an invaluable source of further learning. Special thanks to my husband Dr Mark Sheehan for his help, support and love, and to my father for his encouragement and admirable strength.

# Contents

Introduction   1
1. What is Hypnosis?   3
2. The History of Hypnosis   11
3. How Does Hypnotherapy Work?   19
4. Will Hypnotherapy Work for You?   29
5. Learning Self-Hypnosis   37
6. Practical Therapy for a Range of Problems   53
7. Taking It Further   89
References   91
Further Reading   95
Useful Addresses   97
Index   101

We achieve a sense of self from what we
do for ourselves and how we develop our
capacities. If all your efforts have gone into
developing others, you're bound to feel
empty. TAKE YOUR TURN NOW.

Robin Norwood

# Introduction

The gods help those who help themselves.

Euripides

M Y MAIN MOTIVATION for writing this piece of work has come from the fact that in an otherwise highly edu-cated society, damaging myths about hypnosis still prevail. During the course of this book I hope to dispel these myths, which have their origins in a fascinating history. I will also be exploring the benefits that can be achieved using hypnosis with a wide range of disorders of the body and mind.

Strictly speaking, rather than being a therapy in itself, hypnosis is merely a naturally occurring phenomenon with little known benefit. However, when used as an adjunct to standard psychotherapeutic techniques it becomes very useful indeed. Therefore, in addition to teaching you how to induce self-hypnosis, the further aim of this book will be to introduce you to some of the basic ways in which you can use therapy on yourself in the hypnotic state.

Hypnotherapy is widely used throughout the world by doctors, dentists and psychologists who deem it to be a genuine and effective therapy, often producing profound results. If you wish to contribute to your mental and physical well-being, self-hypnosis will be of definite interest to you.

1

# 1

# What is Hypnosis?

Man cannot discover new oceans
Until he has courage to lose sight of the shore.
Author unidentified

## THE NATURE OF HYPNOSIS

A LOT OF what people believe about hypnosis is untrue, including the idea that its prime function is to entertain. In recent years the use of hypnosis has gained considerable respectability in the medical profession for its therapeutic role in the management of many disorders, both physical and psychological.

### A Definition of Hypnosis

It is difficult to define precisely the nature of hypnosis. For our purposes here it can best be viewed as a state of intense physical and mental relaxation where the subject, although aware of immediate reality, experiences a sense of detachment from it. The focus of attention is usually internal and narrower than when fully alert. As with meditation, hypnosis is claimed to stimulate the right side of the brain, the part responsible for inward awareness, passiveness, feelings of serenity, and floating sensations.

3

## The Conscious and Subconscious Mind

The mind processes information both consciously and subconsciously. The subconscious mind is that part of your mind of which you are unaware. It is in charge of the autonomic nervous system, controlling all involuntary bodily functions, as well as the storing of all your experiences in the form of memories. The deeper part of your mind is responsible also for the entire range of your emotions, ideas, intuition, attitudes, self-image and habits.

When fully alert the conscious mind tends to be very critical and often inclined to over-analyse when problem-solving. This can often lead to unproductive results such as avoidance and indecision, refusal to take action and excessive anxiety. In the hypnotic state, however, the frequently unhelpful conscious mind is less likely to interfere, thus partially freeing the subject from normal logic. This enables the subconscious mind to become more attentive and receptive to therapy in the form of suggestions and imagery. In this way the mind can be positively influenced, allowing work on areas which in the ordinary waking state would usually be out of conscious control. Therapy experienced in the hypnotic state is known as hypnotherapy.

## Comparing Everyday Trances with Formal Hypnosis

A trance is not weird or mysterious. It is a perfectly normal phenomenon, similar to daydreaming or the feeling of drifting before falling asleep. You may often experience hypnosis without realizing it; for example, when driving your car on a familiar journey you may arrive at your destination not remembering everything about the journey. Somewhere along the way your conscious mind drifted away, absorbed in your thoughts, leaving the driving of the car and your safety in the care of your subconscious mind. It can also be experienced when you become so engrossed in a book or television programme that you lose sense of time and forget momentarily where you are.

Certain distinctions can be made between everyday trances and formal hypnosis. With the latter, the hypnotic state and the power of suggestion are used with specific results or goals in mind, with the focus of attention being on inner experiences such as imagery or feelings, rather than in the external world. Otherwise the trances can be highly similar in their subjective nature.

The similarities between familiar everyday trances and formal hypnosis can often lead many people to believe that they have not been in hypnosis, because they have expected the experience to be unique or somehow dramatic. When they have not been 'put under' with their surroundings 'blanked out' they feel disappointed. Such unfounded beliefs and expectations about hypnosis often stem from its use in entertainment and its inaccurate depiction in novels and films.

## SORTING OUT COMMON MISCONCEPTIONS CONCERNING HYPNOSIS

In order to achieve the best results possible from this book it is important that you obtain a reasonable understanding of the topic. It is vital at the outset to dispel the myths and misunderstandings clouding the phenomenon of hypnosis.

### Is Hypnosis Equivalent to Sleep?

Instruments that measure the brain's activity have clearly demonstrated a difference in electroencephalograph (EEG) patterns between sleep and hypnosis. When in a trance state it is thought that you are somewhere between being fully alert and asleep. The deeper into hypnosis you go, the closer you drift towards the state of sleep. In a light state of hypnosis you are nearer to full alertness (see *figure* 1).

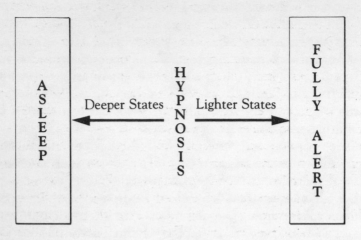

*Figure 1 The trance state is thought to be somewhere between being fully alert and asleep.*

Since you are not asleep you will for the most part remain aware of your surroundings and remember everything about the experience. Amnesia, other than 'normal forgetting', will usually only occur if suggestions to this effect have been given to you.

## Is Depth of Trance Important?

Many patients I deal with in my practice think that unless they feel really 'out of it' during hypnosis the work done with them will not take effect. They are then very pleasantly surprised when they begin to notice positive and often remarkable changes occurring in their lives, regardless of the levels of trance achieved.

It appears that very good work can be done on most areas in light trance states, and therefore time spent being obsessed with achieving deep states of hypnosis is time that could be spent much more productively. It is a little bit like wanting to fill a bucket with water from a well. To achieve your goal it does not matter whether you lower the bucket into the shallow or deep waters of the well. You still end up with the same result – the bucket filled with water!

From observations in my practice, I believe that everyone experiences hypnosis in their own unique way. Some people will slip into deeper trances easier than others. Whichever way works for you, remember that as with any other skill, entering into hypnosis improves with practice. As time moves on you will probably find that on occasions you naturally drift into deeper states. The important point here is not to 'try' to make things happen as this will keep your conscious mind more involved in the process than is desired. Hypnosis involves 'allowing' yourself to let go at your own pace. Always bear in mind that your priority should not be the manner in which you experience hypnosis. Instead, focus on the many benefits you can achieve with the state, regardless of the depth of trance.

## Can the Hypnotist Control the Subject?

Many experts agree with the concept that all hypnosis is self-hypnosis. So although a hypnotist can skilfully help to guide you into a trance, it is only with your permission that the hypnotic state will develop. Nothing will take place without your co-operation and help. When you do eventually drift into hypnosis you will stay completely in control. You will not do anything you do not want to do. Only suggestions that fall within your fundamental interests will be followed through into actual experience.

When in hypnosis, your everyday sense of right and wrong will remain with you. However, even when not in hypnosis, sometimes we can be fooled or tricked by persuasive people into doing something that is not really to our benefit. In theory the same could happen in the presence of an unscrupulous hypnotist. Luckily your chances of meeting someone like that are very low indeed.

It would be wise though, as a general rule of thumb for your protection, never to allow an unqualified person to use hypnosis with you.

Obviously, none of this need concern you when you are practising self-hypnosis, where you are both hypnotist and subject, guiding yourself into the hypnotic state and choosing your own suggestions. Later in this book you will be learning how to ensure these suggestions are as positive and constructive as possible, helping you to bring out the very best in yourself. You will learn, as so many others have before you, how hypnosis, rather than being a process of taking control of people, is a means of empowering individuals, helping them to feel more in command of their own lives.

## Is Hypnosis Dangerous?

Because hypnosis is a naturally occurring state, unlike that induced by certain medications, there are no associated negative side-effects. In fact, once suggestions are kept positive, the only probable side-effects you can expect to experience will be constructive changes in whatever area of your life you choose to work on. It is important to remember, however, that hypnotherapy is not a panacea for every ailment, and should not be used indiscriminately. Neither is it a substitute for tried and tested conventional treatment. However, used appropriately, either on its own or in conjunction with other approaches, hypnotherapy can have a very powerful beneficial effect.

## Can Anyone be Hypnotized?

Most of us have a natural ability to enter into hypnosis to some degree, but there are those who are unhypnotizable, including certain severely disturbed or psychotic individuals and the mentally handicapped. Obviously, people who simply do not wish to be hypnotized will also fall into this category.

Good hypnotic subjects are those who, above all, are willing to experience the trance state. It has also been noted, contrary to popular belief, that weak-minded or gullible persons are more easily hypnotized, that particularly good hypnotic subjects are intelligent with high levels of concentration and vivid imaginations. Whether or not you are a good hypnotic subject should not become the issue, rather, as previously noted, it will be more productive for you to focus on what you want to achieve from utilizing the state to your advantage, whatever level of trance you experience. Above all else, your motivation and desire to effect positive change are most important.

## THE NEGATIVE EFFECTS OF STAGE HYPNOSIS

Many stage hypnotists encourage the myth that, when in hypnosis, the subject is in some way under their control. This can help to create the aura of magic and mystique that is usually vital to the success of these shows. Volunteers deemed to be the most susceptible to hypnosis are selected from the audience and anyone judged to be 'resisting' is quickly dismissed. As we have already noted, because no one can be hypnotized without giving consent, those who remain on stage are individuals who really want to be up there and who are very willing to be a part of the show.

Whether hypnotized or not, there is intense pressure from the hypnotist and the audience to 'go along with things' so that everyone can have an entertaining evening. As the stage hypnotist 'takes responsibility' for the actions of the volunteers, this offers them a licence to let go of their inhibitions. Any unacceptable behaviour can be blamed on 'the power' of the hypnotist, in the same way that people blame a few drinks for behaviour they would later prefer was forgotten!

Clinical hypnosis is very different from stage hypnosis –

there are no Elvis Presley impressions done in my office! The sad fact is that, although stage hypnosis may be entertaining and without doubt keeps the phenomenon of hypnosis alive in the public eye, it also does a lot of damage to the further promotion of hypnotherapy in medicine. It clouds the true value of hypnosis.

While in some countries the practice of stage hypnosis is a criminal offence, at the time of writing such shows are thriving in Britain. Many patients come to my office either terrified that I will control them in some way or expecting a complete miracle cure in one session because of some form of 'magic' or 'power' they feel I possess. The myths that so desperately need to be overthrown will continue to prosper as long as hypnosis is allowed to be used in entertainment.

# 2

# The History of Hypnosis

All sciences alike have descended from magic and superstition, but none has been so slow as hypnosis in shaking off the evil associations of its origins.

Clark Hull

THE INTENTIONAL AND ACCIDENTAL practice of hypnosis can be found in various forms throughout the past. It has often been associated with faith healing, magic, and the supernatural. Although the word 'hypnosis' was coined only in the last century, its history is probably as long as that of mankind.

Many of the world's most ancient civilizations, including the ancient Egyptians, Persians, Greeks and Romans, recognized the power of suggestion and the usefulness of the hypnotic state. However, benefits achieved were generally attributed to miracles, believed to have been carried out by the gods. The earliest medical records describe inexplicable healing by oracles in the 'sleep temples' of Greece. People would come to these temples to put forward petitions and receive interpretations of dreams, which were more than likely hypnotically induced.

Because hypnosis as a specific therapy dates from the 18th century, it is not necessary for our purposes to delve into ancient history. The following historical review will begin with more modern times.

11

## THE ORIGINS OF MODERN HYPNOSIS: FRANZ ANTON MESMER (1734–1815)

Modern-day hypnotism is believed to have originated from the work of a flamboyant Austrian doctor named Mesmer. He believed that an invisible magnetic fluid emerged from the stars and influenced people's health. When there was an imbalance in the flow of this fluid, disease would occur. The appropriate flow between the patient and the planets was restored by rubbing the afflicted person's body with magnets, redistributing the fluid and thus restoring health. In time Mesmer found that he could produce the same benefits by passing his hands over his patients. He attributed this to the 'animal magnetism' he possessed in his own body and hands.

In 1778, at the invitation of King Louis XVI, Mesmer went to Paris. He was so popular there that it soon became impossible for him to continue treating patients individually. It was at this point that he devised his famous 'baquets'. These were large tubs filled with water and iron filings from which protruded iron rods. These rods were clasped by patients so they could receive the 'magnetic flow'. Quite the showman, Mesmer would dress up in flowing lilac garments for these occasions with what resembled a wand in his hand!

In a dimly lit treatment room with soft music and reflecting mirrors, patients would hold hands in a circle while Mesmer moved from person to person. The majority of his patients were female and his approach was frequently rather sexual, involving a lot of touching and stroking. Sometimes the patient's knees would be held between his own during treatment, resulting in the lower parts of their bodies being in close proximity. Mesmer's method was considered particularly outrageous in an era when doctors were not permitted to listen to a woman's heartbeat for fear they might touch her breast.

Much to the irritation of the medical profession at the time, Mesmer was curing a great many people whom doctors had long given up on. A commission to investigate 'mesmerism' was appointed by the King in 1784. Its finding stated that the cures were due to the patients' belief and imagination and not to magnetism. The focus on, and adverse reaction to, Mesmer's theories and theatrical way of conducting treatment meant that a crucial point was overlooked. The fact was that sometimes noticeable positive changes did occur in patients – the use of the imagination could indeed be curative. Charles d'Eslon, a pupil of Mesmer, had already remarked: 'If the medicine of imagination is best, why should we not practise the medicine of imagination?' This plea was to fall on deaf ears for many years to follow.

What investigators, or indeed Mesmer himself, did not realize was that during treatment patients were more than likely entering into a hypnotic state. This was not due to the effects of 'magnetism' *per se*; rather it was as a result of the way Mesmer conducted treatment and the rituals involved in the method. Also, strong suggestions of some kind of mysterious power were present, as were either direct or indirect suggestions that healing would occur.

Mesmer's part in the history of hypnotism was a vital one, for he created interest in an area which was afterwards to be followed through and refined by others, ultimately leading to the practice of hypnosis as we know it today.

## THE MARQUIS ARMAND DE PUYSÉGUR
## (1751–1825)

Puységur was a retired military man who studied under Mesmer. His historical importance lies in his observation and labelling of people who nowadays would be categorized as being extremely susceptible to hypnosis. Puységur noticed that such individuals could enter a deep trance state which came to be known as 'artificial somnambulism' or a 'sleeping' trance. Unfortunately, this helped to give a basis to the mistaken idea that hypnosis is the same as sleep. During this period, due to the unyielding resistance of doctors, mesmerism was for the most part merely a curiosity demonstrated by showmen at travelling fairs.

## JOHN ELLIOTSON (1791–1868)
## AND JAMES ESDAILE (1808–1859)

Still strongly against the practice of mesmerism, the medical profession ensured that Elliotson, a physician, was dismissed from his professional post at the University College Hospital in London when they learned he was using this method to perform painless surgery. Elliotson, having introduced the stethoscope to England, was sufficiently respected to attract enough support subsequently to establish his own hospital in Fitzroy Square and start a journal called *The Zoist*, which dealt with issues of mesmerism.

Strongly influenced by Elliotson's work, Esdaile, a Scottish surgeon practising in India, used mesmerism to perform over 300 major operations without pain. The most common of these involved the excision of massive scrotal tumours, although 19 amputations are also recorded! With the development of chemical anaesthetics – nitrous oxide in 1844 and ether in 1846 – the use of mesmerism for surgical purposes declined.

## JAMES BRAID (1795–1860)

It was at this crucial point that interest in mesmerism was revived by a surgeon from Edinburgh named Braid. He merits the title 'The Father of Modern Hypnotism' since it was he who changed the name from mesmerism to 'hypnotism'. The word 'hypnosis' is derived from the Greek word 'hypnos' meaning sleep. Later, Braid recognized that hypnosis was not sleep, but the name stuck.

This new name managed to dissociate Braid's work in

this area from the activities of his predecessors, which most medical men had frowned on and viewed as unprofessional. This, combined with the fact that Braid was an accepted and conservative member of the medical profession, placing emphasis on a scientific approach, allowed hypnosis for the first time ever to come somewhere close to being considered reputable.

Braid was the first to put forward the idea that the hypnotic state could be achieved without the involvement of magnetic fluids. Rather than affecting the body directly, he believed that the hypnotist was influencing the subject by suggestion alone. Therefore, he came to the conclusion that the phenomenon of hypnotism depended on the subject's suggestibility as opposed to any necessity for the hypnotist to possess 'magical powers'. Using a hypnotic induction, which became known as 'Braidism', he would ask his patients to concentrate their gaze on a single point while he gave the appropriate suggestions.

## AMBROSE-AUGUST LIÉBEAULT (1823–1904)
## HIPPOLYTE-MARIE BERNHEIM (1837–1919)
## JEAN MARTIN CHARCOT (1825–1893)

Hypnotism was widely studied and practised throughout the second half of the 19th century. Some of the contributors of that time particularly stand out for their influence. Liébeault, a general practitioner at Nancy in France, used hypnosis extensively in his work. He was never short of subjects as he would give patients free treatment, as long as they agreed to accept a hypnotic approach in place of the more conventional methods of the time, where appropriate. Bernheim, a famous neurologist, on travelling to Liébeault's clinic to prove him a fraud, was so fascinated by his work that he susequently became involved with Liébeault in the foundation of the 'Nancy School Of Hypnosis'.

Around the same time in France, Charcot, also a neurologist, proclaimed that hypnotizability was the product of an abnormal nervous make-up. This was in opposition to the view held by Bernheim and Liébeault who believed, as we do today, that hypnosis is a naturally occurring everyday state and 'normal' subjects are equally hypnotizable. Although Charcot's theories did not become part of the more modern view of hypnosis, the fact that such a highly esteemed medical authority considered hypnotism worthy of study added weight to the earlier efforts of Braid to make hypnosis respectable and acceptable to the medical profession.

## SIGMUND FREUD (1856–1939)

At the close of the 19th century, having studied under both Charcot and Bernheim, Freud began to use hypnosis with patients in his native Austria. He was one of the first to utilize hypnosis to investigate the subconscious mind for possible causes of anxiety. Prior to this the main emphasis had been on removal of direct symptoms rather than elimination of apparent causes.

Freud ultimately became disillusioned with hypnosis when he found that not all patients were willing to follow this method or capable of being hypnotized to the depth necessary for the work he wished to carry out, and that results were not always permanent. Instead, he developed an approach involving free association and dream interpretation which became known as psychoanalysis. Whereas modern hypnotherapy can bring about positive change in a relatively short period of time, psychoanalysis can often take years.

## THE DRAMATIC RISE OF HYPNOSIS

In 1891 the British Medical Association appointed a committee to investigate the nature and value of hypnotism. The report that followed declared acceptance of hypnotic phenomena as genuine, and satisfaction that hypnotism could be of use in the therapeutic process. It also advised against its use for the purpose of entertainment. However, despite the positive results of the enquiry, interest in hypnosis continued to wane, both in Britain and abroad. In particular, Freud's abandonment of the approach would appear to have created an immense setback. With very few exceptions, hypnosis fell into misuse once more in the hands of charlatans and entertainers, further discouraging professionals from becoming associated with it.

It was not until the First World War, when the need arose for rapid treatment of battle neuroses, that hypnotism received a revival in attention. Hypnotherapy proved very valuable in this area, and so was back in the spotlight again. While most of the early work was carried out by doctors, the advent of the science of psychology in the 20th century led to the increased role of psychologists in the process of placing hypnotism under scientific scrutiny. The first modern book on the topic was by Clark L Hull (1884–1952) in 1933, and was entitled *Hypnosis and Suggestibility: An Experimental Approach*.

Following the publication of Hull's classic work, the literature began to expand rapidly and continues to do so to this day. In 1953 the British Medical Association, in a report from an appointed committee, officially sanctioned the use of hypnosis to treat both physical and psychological disorders. The American Medical Association gave its approval three years later.

From a historical viewpoint, while many medical and psychological fads have come and gone, hypnosis has always survived. Today, despite its continued misuse in entertainment, scientific interest in hypnosis has never been more alive. Long may hypnotherapy continue to enhance and play a significant role in medicine!

# 3

# How Does Hypnotherapy Work?

*Thou shalt decree a thing, and it shall be established unto thee.*
                                                        Job 22:28

THOSE WHO ARE QUICK to criticize hypnosis often point out that no one knows exactly how it works. This is indeed true. However, it is not necessary to understand the mechanism of how something works in order to derive the benefits of its action. For instance, many of us do not know how our bodies digest food, yet that does not stop us taking food in and absorbing it. Similarly, a lot of us do not comprehend the workings of an engine, but this does not prevent us from driving a car.

Hypnosis is widely utilized in the therapy situation because time and time again its beneficial effects have been recorded. Since, for the most part, the precise manner in which it operates remains a mystery, my main focus in this chapter will be on providing a description of the effects of hypnotherapy. In order to do this, it is useful to begin with an examination of the relationship between the mind and body.

## THE MIND/BODY RELATIONSHIP

Since ancient times man has been curious about the manner in which the mind and body co-exist. While many have put forward the idea that they operate separately, more recent

19

thought and research on the subject have moved towards the belief that they work in unison. This has led to the development of 'holistic medicine', which views the human being as an integrated 'whole'.

Many examples of the close relationship between body and mind can be seen in our everyday lives. The effect that physical processes can have on the mind is clearly noticed, for instance, when coffee containing caffeine is consumed. Caffeine is a stimulant of the central nervous system and thereby increases levels of concentration and alertness. Excessive intake of caffeine can lead to moods of anxiety. Also, in medicine many useful drugs can alter the mental processes – for example, anxiolytic agents such as the benzodiazepines can be temporarily used to affect negative emotions in a positive way.

Similarly, mental and emotional experiences can be seen to produce definite reactions in the body. For instance, if you become scared or anxious many things can happen. Your sympathetic nervous system is activated within your body, resulting in a release of adrenaline from your adrenal glands into your blood stream and a quickening of your respiration and heart rate. Blood flow is diverted from areas such as the bowel and skin to tissue like muscle, heart and lung. The net effect is to prepare you to take 'action' and be 'alert'. On the other hand, if you are thinking pleasant thoughts and feeling calm, your body will be more relaxed, with your breathing slow and even and your heart beating at a normal pace.

Hypnotherapy employs this notion that the processes of the mind have a direct effect on the body. It is not necessary for our purposes to delve into a detailed world of biochemistry and neurophysiology; suffice it to say that when in hypnosis, it would appear that a basic form of biological communication occurs via the release of biochemical transmitters in the body.

For example, Rossi and Cheek (1988), reviewing the relevant literature, conclude that evidence is accumulating that 'mind/body' methods such as hypnotherapy can alter the experience of pain at all major levels of information transduction in the body. At the 'mind/brain' level, it has been found that in hypnosis many subjects are able to 'distort' their own perception so that they experience deep levels of hypnotic anaesthesia (Orne, 1976; McGlashan et al, 1969). At the 'brain/body' level, increases in endorphins (the body's own natural pain killer) have been recorded following hypnotherapy (Kaji et al, 1981; Domangue et al, 1985). Finally, at what is termed the 'cellular/genetic' level, hypnotic suggestion has been related to measurable changes in tissue vulnerability (Chapman et al, 1959). Biochemical transmitters appear to work to reduce pain and promote healing.

It becomes clear that by working on the mind and producing changes in it we can expect the person as a whole to be influenced at many levels. This premise rests at the very core of the workings of hypnotherapy.

## MAKING YOUR MIND WORK TO YOUR ADVANTAGE

In chapter 1 it was noted that suggestions in hypnosis appear to go directly to the subconscious mind for the most part, bypassing the conscious analytical and critical process. This is obviously beneficial since constructive and positive suggestions can reach that part of the mind which, like a creative child, is versatile enough to receive, explore and elaborate on these positive guidelines. This can often result in a reorganization of information in the mind. However, what a lot of people do not realize is that you do not have to be in the hypnotic state to take suggestions on board. It appears true that suggestibility increases in hypnosis, but you are also open to suggestion when fully alert.

You are constantly giving yourself suggestions. It is claimed that information from the conscious mind slips directly into the subconscious mind. So every conscious thought contributes to the building of the deeper part of your mind. This means that the effects of hypnotherapy and self-hypnosis over time are going to be very much dependent on the kind of everyday suggestions you pass to your subconscious mind through your thoughts influencing your belief system. Therefore it is important when studying the workings of hypnotherapy and suggestion to include some background on the concept of positive thinking.

## The Power of Suggestion

When you feed suggestions into the subconscious mind it can very much be a case of 'what you put in is what you may get out'. If you allow your thoughts to be negative, this can lead to negative feelings, attitudes and beliefs. On the other hand, making your thoughts positive can create a sense of well-being. You own your thoughts, so you can control them. It sounds simple, but it produces results – when you change the way you think you can change the way you feel.

If you have fallen into the habit of thinking in a negative way, how can you change this? I usually give patients the following task, which works in two ways: firstly, it helps to break the habit of negative thinking, and secondly, as the technique is repeatedly practised, it encourages the new habit of positive thinking. Anything you repeat often enough can become automatic. Starting today, become aware of how you are allowing yourself to think and whenever you entertain a negative thought, think 'stop' or see a 'stop' road sign in your mind. Then, dealing directly with the subject matter, change the negative focus of your thoughts into a positive one. Make the very best of reality as it is (see *figure 2*). If the habit of negative thinking is deeply engrained, you will need to do this exercise persistently and aggressively over time.

It can also be useful whenever possible to keep the words in your suggestions positive, as well as the meaning of the complete sentence. For instance, if someone was to think, 'I

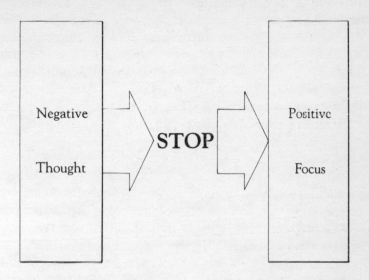

*Figure 2 The 'stop' technique to combat negative thinking*

am not feeling anxious and nervous about the party tonight,' the very fact that the words 'anxious and nervous' have been fed into their subconscious mind could result in that person feeling ill-at-ease, even though the meaning of the thought as a whole was positive. It would be more helpful to think about the party using positive words such as:' I can feel relaxed and confident about the party tonight.'

It also makes sense to eliminate such words as 'try' or 'hope' when constructing suggestions. Such words can imply failure or doubt to your mind. So, for example, avoid saying, 'I am trying to work at being a more positive person,' or 'I am hoping to work at being a more positive person.' A suggestion such as 'I am working at being a more positive person' will be much more powerful.

It is only through perseverance, through supporting positive sets of possibilities proposed in hypnosis with positive suggestions in your everyday thinking, that a reserve of positivity can be created. In time the deeper part of your mind can be persuaded to allow a new, more positive outlook to predominate in your subconscious. For suggestions to work, their repetition, in and out of hypnosis, is the key. The more positive thoughts you put into your mind the better. In time your beliefs can alter and your goals of realistic positive change can seem that much more attainable.

As well as working to keep your everyday thoughts positive, another way you can powerfully extend your self-hypnosis work is to use what are known as post-hypnotic suggestions. These suggestions employ the naturally occurring talent of the mind to link things together and make associations. Post-hypnotic suggestions can be defined as suggestions given while in the hypnotic state which work by associating a specific trigger with a specific desired response which will take place after the trance experience.

For instance, a businessman wishing to improve his confidence when speaking in front of his colleagues may suggest to himself in hypnosis beforehand: 'As I enter the boardroom I can feel calmly confident.' The post-hypnotic cue of entering the boardroom can then initiate or trigger the response of calm confidence in that person when he most needs it. Similarly, those wishing to become slimmer and cut down on unnecessary snacking between meals may suggest the following to themselves: 'As I approach the fridge door I can notice how comfortably full my stomach feels.'

## The Importance of the Imagination

In addition to working in a positive way with verbal suggestions, your imagination can be utilized very much to your advantage. It was Einstein who claimed that imagination is more important than knowledge. In particular, the use of imagery is a very powerful means of working on yourself, whether you are fully alert or practising self-hypnosis. Imagery is often claimed to be the language of the deeper part of the mind.

Figure 3 *Practise in your imagination what you want rather than what you do not want.*

Using your imagination in a positive way can help to improve your performance at anything you do. Prather (1973) found that trainee pilots using mental practice of manoeuvres for landing aircraft were rated better in their landing-skill proficiency than trainees who did not use this method. This demonstrates how practising in your imagination (a process known as 'mental rehearsal' or 'imaginal rehearsal') can produce outstanding results. It can put a positive map in your mind to follow.

I once worked with a woman who came to see me because although she had the skill to pass her driving test she had a history of failing it. She described to me how uptight she would feel for weeks preceding the test, and how on the day itself she would be consumed with panic and unable to do herself justice. On questioning her further it was revealed that whenever she thought about the driving test she would imagine herself looking panicky and doing everything wrong. She had not only failed the test on three occasions in reality, but also about a thousand times in her imagination! In effect, although she desperately wanted to pass, in her imagination she was helping to impress on her subconscious mind a negative attitude regarding the test, ultimately reducing her chances of success. Over the coming weeks I gave her the task of rehearsing repeatedly and persistently in her mind the way she would like her test to go, seeing herself looking and feeling calm and confident and everything going the very best way realistically possible. The next time she took her driving test she found that everything went just as she had planned in her imagination and she passed. Since the effect of the imagination appears more powerful than the will, it is important that your imagination works in the same direction as your desires.

Your imagination can also be used to control negative feelings. If you were watching a horror movie containing one horrific scene after another, the chances are you would have an unpleasant feeling inside. Alternatively, viewing a film showing breathtaking scenes of beautiful places may help you to feel at ease. 'Pictures' or 'ideas' you allow yourself to sense in your mind's eye can work in a similar way.

The notion of perceptions in your mind working to alter your feelings can prove very useful. An overstressed patient of mine found he could effectively calm himself if he chose to imagine himself sitting on a balcony in Spain, his favourite holiday spot. He had such a good imagination he could almost feel he was really there. Another patient with osteoarthritis in her knees found heat usually soothed her pain, so she would imagine that she was sitting in her garden with the sun's rays concentrating on her knees. In time, during this exercise she could actually feel her knees becoming warmer, and her pain would ease dramatically. With practice, a poor imagination can be trained and developed to work in this beneficial way (See the section entitled 'Exploring your imagination' in chapter 5.)

Imagery for altering how you feel can also be utilized in a symbolic way by visualizing unwanted feelings in some tangible form and then modifying or disposing of the image created. For instance, a patient suffering from migraine imagined the feeling of pain in a visual way as a tight, iron hat on her head. When she imagined loosening the grip of the hat or taking it off, she found in time that her headache would ease and sometimes even disappear completely. People wishing to feel calmer could, for example, imagine their anxious feelings being represented by rubbish which is thrown on a fire and quickly burns away.

Imagery, as well as being used in a positive way to work on performance and feelings or sensations in the body, can also be used to modify certain bodily functions. For instance, appropriate use of the imagination in hypnosis as soon as possible after experiencing a burn can reduce the likelihood of inflammation and blistering (Ewin, 1979). Patients can visualize ice-cold water flowing over the affected area and that part of the body then looking cool and healed. The successful impact of the imagination in hypnosis on controlling vascular flow has also been documented (Bishay and Lee, 1984). Patients suffering from high blood pressure, for example, could imagine travelling through the arteries of their body in a canoe. They could then visualize these arteries becoming wider and subsequently the blood flowing more freely and rapidly.

To summarize, as well as being the fundamental tools for creating and sustaining the hypnotic state, suggestions and imagery are the mode used to treat a wide range of areas which can benefit from therapeutic intervention. Hypnotherapy appears to work by encouraging the utilization of the patients' inner resources. Subconscious problem-solving and healing processes can be encouraged to operate to some degree free from conscious, learned limitations. The therapeutic effect is experienced not only in the mind; rather, as a result of what appears to be the biological communication of information in the body, the whole person can benefit.

# 4

# Will Hypnotherapy Work for You?

You will have wonderful surges forward. Then there must be a
time of consolidation before the next forward surge. Accept this
as part of the process and never become downhearted.

Eileen Caddy

M ANY OF THOSE SEEKING hypnotherapy as a treatment are
often looking for a magical cure that will not involve
any effort on their part. These people have believed the
myths of hypnosis, including the many extravagant claims
made in the past regarding its effectiveness in treating any
and every condition. The reality is that hypnotherapy
achieves a range of different results with patients.

It is true that many people can be dramatically helped
with hypnotherapy, obtaining the types of changes they
were hoping for. They often view such results as 'amazing'
and 'incredible' – even 'magical'! However, there are some
people who will only gain minimum benefit, and others
who may not notice any change at all following therapy.
Hypnotherapy does not vary in this respect from any other
mode of treatment available.

It seems reasonable that variable outcomes can be
recorded when different patients are being treated for different conditions. However, discrepancies are also recorded in
results when patients have been treated with the same techniques, for the same 'condition' and by the same therapist.
Many factors can influence the success of therapy. These
include the patient having realistic expectations, wanting
things to change, having clear goals, being committed to

working on himself or herself, and keeping a diary. We will explore these factors in detail and it will become clearer what you need to do to ensure that you end up in the camp of those who benefit greatly from this therapeutic approach.

## HAVING REALISTIC EXPECTATIONS

As stated in chapter 1, hypnotherapy should never be considered to be a substitute for conventional medicine. Also, it is necessary to realize that it is not a panacea for every ailment. Sometimes certain facts of life are unchangeable. For example, certain medical conditions are irreversible and it would be completely unrealistic to attempt to 'cure' them using hypnotherapy. The best that may be realistically aimed at in the management of such disorders would be the controlling of symptoms of discomfort, and this would require regular work in self-hypnosis for a long time.

Many patients can also have unrealistic expectations regarding the duration of treatment. Sometimes they expect a 'one-session cure' from hypnotherapy even though they have been attending a doctor or psychologist for several years for the same condition without success. Whatever you wish to work on in self-hypnosis, it is of vital importance that your expectation regarding the rate at which you benefit is realistic. Otherwise you will easily become discouraged.

Be patient! It has probably taken your whole life to create your mind as it functions at present – it may need some time to change. Improvement usually tends to be a gradual process and may be interspersed with occasions when little benefit is noticed, or there may even be a recurrence of your 'symptoms'. Although there will be times when your progress may appear static, it should not be long before things will move forward in a positive way once more, provided you continue to work on yourself.

## WANTING THINGS TO CHANGE

It is essential when practising self-hypnosis that you really want the changes you are working for and that you have the motivation to succeed. It can be useful at the outset to list as many benefits as possible that you hope to obtain on achieving your goal of positive change. For example, if you were wishing to work on reaching your ideal weight you could note that on achieving this goal you would:

- feel healthier
- be more comfortable with yourself
- feel more confident and attractive
- have a wider range of clothes to choose from
- be more mobile
- find exercise more enjoyable
- be inclined to socialize more
- feel proud of yourself for being in control of food

Making yourself fully aware of all these benefits can strengthen your motivation and desire to change even further.

Once you have explored the benefits of change it is then worth examining any benefits, or 'secondary gains' as they are often called, you may be experiencing from your present situation. Secondary gain can be defined as benefit you are achieving from an otherwise aggravating situation or behaviour. A person may or may not be conscious of such benefits. These gains can often help to keep a person 'locked' in an undesirable predicament. Until they are addressed and satisfied in other more appropriate ways, secondary gains can make it difficult for someone to move forward in a positive way.

For instance, I once had a patient who wished to become a non-smoker. When we probed into the area of possible secondary gains she may be obtaining from her habit, it transpired that she used the action of going out for a cigarette to avoid dealing with negative emotions. In particular, whenever she was in conflict with her husband, rather than sort out their differences and contend with the further upset this would initially entail, she would leave the room and have a cigarette to 'help suppress her anger'. Until this patient could learn to deal with negative emotions in another more appropriate way it was going to be difficult for her to become a non-smoker. This was the main area therapy focused on in helping her to become free from cigarettes.

If you have worked with self-hypnosis on some area of your life for some time, but are still no nearer to achieving your goals, it may well be that there are some benefits to your situation and/or underlying reasons for your behaviour that you are not consciously aware of and which need to be addressed. One method often used to uncover such information has been outlined by Bresler (1990). The approach is known as 'the inner adviser technique'. It involves giving voice and form to your subconscious mind or inner wisdom in your imagination when in a comfortable, relaxed state. (See the next chapter for suggestions on how to achieve this state.) For example, I visualize my own 'inner adviser' as a wise old man similar in appearance to a picture I saw in a children's book of 'Merlin the Magician' many years ago!

Once you have introduced yourself to the 'inner adviser' in your mind, you can then ask whether he/she is willing to help you with the problem in hand. If the reply to this question is positive you can ask whatever questions you feel are appropriate to help enhance insight into possible underlying reasons for the behaviour and into any secondary gains. You may find it useful when posing questions to ask them on your out breath (exhalation). The first response entering your mind on your in breath (inhalation) can then be taken as your adviser's reply. Sometimes the adviser may act in a protective manner, not responding to your questions if he/she feels you are not ready to handle the replies at a conscious level. If this happens it may be useful to ask your adviser what you need to do in order to be in a better position to receive such information. At this point, help from a trained therapist may also be required to shine some further light on the area.

Some people will be reluctant to let go of the secondary gains of their problem behaviour or unwilling to find other more appropriate ways of achieving these benefits. They may also be uncomfortable with the idea of confronting and dealing with any possible underlying problems influencing their behaviour. Such persons will have very low motivation to change.

## CLARIFYING YOUR GOALS

When commencing a journey it is useful to know exactly where you want to go! Before working on yourself in self-hypnosis it is helpful to be clear on what you wish for yourself and to believe it is within your capabilities to achieve it. As well as being realistic, it is helpful to ensure that your goals are specific and well thought out.

For instance, if you wish to become a more confident person, think about what being confident would mean for you. Imagine specific situations, seeing the way you would wish to act and the qualities you would like to possess. Some people find it useful to think of a role model who exemplifies the desired behaviour. This role model can be someone you know or a person you can create in your imagination.

Clarifying your goals enables the subconscious mind to have as much information as possible regarding what you wish to accomplish. It can greatly facilitate the structuring of appropriate clear suggestions and can also help you to identify positive changes more easily as they begin to happen. This can keep you motivated in your work on yourself.

Sometimes it may be appropriate to break a main goal down into a number of steps. For example, it is more appropriate for an agoraphobic to aim at the goal of feeling comfortable walking to the front gate, before moving on to the next goal of feeling happy to walk around the block, and so on. The ultimate and main goal would be to live a 'normal' life (having first clarified exactly what that would mean). Breaking goals into digestible steps gives the subconscious mind not only reasonable targets to aim for but also the opportunity for many intermediate successes along the way.

## BEING COMMITTED TO WORKING ON YOURSELF

To obtain maximum benefit from self-hypnosis you will need to put in a lot of time and effort. You are the one who will make the positive changes happen. This means that you will have to be very committed to your goals. You will need to make self-hypnosis a regular part of your life, so it is worth taking the time to tailor the techniques of this book to your preferences, making their practice as enjoyable as possible. To begin with you will probably need to work on yourself daily.

Often people tell me how busy they are and that their lifestyle does not allow them time for practising self-hypnosis. These same persons usually have time to watch television or take a break with a cup of coffee! Everyone has some bit of spare time – no matter how short it may be. People who are 'too busy' are really saying that practising self-hypnosis is not a top priority for them at this time. Your commitment to working on yourself will very much depend on how much it is worth to you to achieve and then maintain positive change.

## HAVING SUPPORT FROM THOSE AROUND YOU

Another important factor affecting positive change can be the type of support you get from family and friends. It makes the passage a lot easier if people encourage and reinforce your efforts to change in a positive way. Sometimes, however, even though change is to your benefit, there can be an initial negative response from those around you. For example, you may meet with disapproval if in the past you have been a 'doormat' but are now suddenly starting to become more assertive, expressing needs and demands of your own! If you find yourself in such a position do not get downhearted. Just as you will need to become accustomed to change, so too will your family and friends need time to adapt.


## KEEPING A DIARY

Monitoring and keeping records of your therapeutic activities can increase the likelihood of keeping to your planned programme of action. It can be also useful to record how you are positively progressing over time as you continue to work on yourself. For example, if your goal is to become a more relaxed person you could include in your diary a note of those situations or incidents that you feel you are handling in a calmer way than you would have done in the past. Recording the beneficial effects of your work in this way will encourage you and increase your faith in what you are doing.

Whether used on its own or as an adjunct to other treatment, hypnotherapy and self-hypnosis can benefit most people in one way or another. To make it work, however, *you* will need to work. The best results will be achieved by those who are well motivated and determined to make things better.

Like anything else in life in which you invest serious effort, commitment to therapy can reap very powerful rewards. It is within your grasp. All you have to do is decide you will take control. You can make a difference. This book could be the start of a brand new life. It is up to you to create change. As Goethe put it: 'Whatever you can do, or dream you can . . . begin it. Boldness has genius, power and magic in it. Begin it now.' Know you deserve better and go for it!

# 5

# Learning Self-Hypnosis

You didn't think when you got up this morning that this would
be the day your life would change, did you? But it's going to
happen because the only thing that stands between you and
grand success in living are these two things: Getting started and
never quitting!

Robert H Schuller

A S STATED AT THE BEGINNING of this book, many experts
agree that all hypnosis is self-hypnosis. For our purposes
here, however, when we speak of self-hypnosis we are
referring to a person practising hypnotherapy on themselves
without the assistance of a hypnotherapist. This chapter is
broken down into four sections. Firstly, I will outline some
precautions in using hypnosis. Then many practical issues
regarding the practice of self-hypnosis will be discussed. A
short section on how to relax will follow before a final
look at a number of hypnotic inductions for the purpose
of self-hypnosis.

Because you will be acting as therapist as well as subject
during the course of your self-hypnosis, you will require a
necessary amount of active participation from your conscious
mind. This can mean that you may not experience as deep a
state of hypnosis as if you visited a hypnotherapist. However,
practice will improve this situation. Indeed, dramatic hypnotic
effects have been recorded with the use of self-hypnosis. For
example, a dental surgeon named Victor Raush (1980) successfully utilized self-hypnosis as the only method of inducing
anaesthesia when undergoing a gall-bladder operation! Most

people can learn to use self-hypnosis to help them to realize their full potential in all aspects of their lives.

## PRECAUTIONS WHEN USING HYPNOSIS

1 Avoid self-hypnosis and hypnotherapy if you have a history of epilepsy. There is a slim chance that the altered state of hypnosis might induce a fit.
2 Never practise self-hypnosis while involved in any activity requiring you to be alert, for instance, driving.
3 If you intend to drive after a self-hypnosis session, ensure that you are feeling fully alert.

## PRACTICAL ISSUES

### *Where to Practise Self-Hypnosis*

Most people, particularly to begin with, will probably find it easiest to practise self-hypnosis indoors in a quiet room. Wherever you choose, it is important to feel comfortable and safe, ensuring as much as possible that you will not be disturbed. If you are practising at home it is useful to take the phone off the hook and to let members of the household know that you are taking some special time for yourself.

Although many people enjoy a session of self-hypnosis in bed before going to sleep, the risk here, of course, is that you could fall asleep! If you wish specifically to work on helping yourself to sleep, obviously this will be appropriate. However, if you want to focus on some other area of your life, falling asleep will mean that you are no longer actively involved in working on yourself. For this reason I usually recommend that patients avoid lying down when practising self-hypnosis. Remember, you wish to be somewhere in between being asleep and awake, not completely in slumberland! A comfortable chair allowing appropriate support for your head can work well in this respect. If you feel more at ease with your feet up you may like to use a footstool or another chair. The focus should be on comfort.

### The Best Time to Work on Yourself

There are no set rules about which time of the day will be most suitable for your self-hypnosis session. It will very much depend on your schedule. Usually it becomes a case of practising when you have the time and the inclination to take a break. For instance, many people favour the evening, when the chores and demands of the day have come to an end. If there are children in the house you may want to wait until they are in bed and the house is quiet and free from distraction.

Many of my patients over the years have found it beneficial to practise self-hypnosis at approximately the same time each day. They have claimed that it makes entering the hypnotic state that bit easier each time. The reasoning behind this probably rests on the fact that the mind can easily become conditioned to certain rituals of behaviour in our lives. Just as you can get into the habit of feeling hungry as you approach the time you usually have a meal, so too can you train your mind to begin feeling more relaxed in anticipation of the time allotted for a session of self-hypnosis. In time, your mind associates that part of the day with feelings of peace and serenity.

Such an effect can be further reinforced with the repetitive use of an appropriate post-hypnotic suggestion. As previously stated in chapter 3, this is a suggestion given while in the hypnotic state to trigger a desired response to take place after the hypnotic experience. For example, you could suggest the following to yourself: 'Each day as 8 o'clock approaches I can notice how, if I wish to practise self-hypnosis, I will become as comfortable and relaxed as I feel now.' The post-hypnotic cue of 8 o'clock can then trigger the response of comfort and relaxation, facilitating the ease with which you slip into hypnosis. However, it is important to put quality time aside for self-hypnosis – not just what's 'left-over'.

## Length of Time to Spend in Hypnosis

I usually advise patients new to self-hypnosis to practise initially for 20 to 30 minutes a day. As your skill at entering the trance state increases and you become more familiar with the whole process, you will find yourself focusing more on the therapy side of things as less time is required to settle into hypnosis. At this stage you may wish to shorten your sessions to 10 to 15 minutes. However, since the experience of being in hypnosis is usually so pleasant and comfortable, people tend very much to enjoy spending time in this tranquil state of mind and generally are not in any rush to come out! This is good news, of course, because the more time you spend repeating your suggestions in hypnosis, the better.

Now and again in the past I have had patients who have expressed a fear of becoming 'locked in hypnosis'. These people were afraid that if they practised self-hypnosis they might end up drifting in the hypnotic state for days or even weeks! This is no more likely to occur than becoming locked in the state of sleep. The worst that could happen if you were tired during your self-hypnosis is that you could fall asleep and therefore spend more time relaxing than first intended. If this were ever to happen to you, chances are your body needed the extra sleep and in time you would awaken feeling pleasantly refreshed.

If you wish to ensure a limit to the length of time you spend in your session of relaxation you may decide, in a similar fashion to waking yourself from sleep in the morning, to use an alarm clock to bring you out of the hypnotic state. The effect will feel very much the same. I have spoken to many people who find that they can programme themselves to wake out of sleep a few minutes before their alarm clock goes off in the morning. I know I can quite easily do this myself by telling myself the night before what time I wish to awaken. It always intrigues me that for this to happen some part of the mind must count up all the seconds, minutes and hours!

Similarly, when you are practising your self-hypnosis you could suggest to your mind before you close your eyes the time you wish to open them again. It is amazing how accurate your mind can be. In time, like many of my patients, you may come to trust your skill in this respect to such an extent that you no longer feel the need to bother with an alarm clock.

## How to Deal with Distractions

As stated earlier, it is easiest to practise self-hypnosis in an environment free from disturbances and distractions. However, perhaps not all of you have access to such a perfect place and therefore will have a certain amount of unavoidable outside noise to contend with. One way of dealing with this can be to play relaxing music throughout your self-hypnosis, listening to the soothing notes through headphones if possible. This can often be enough to shut out distracting sounds.

However, if certain outside sounds are still filtering through, rather than attempting to ignore them you can decide to use them to your advantage. For example, you could link positive suggestions for relaxation to these noises in the following way: 'As I hear the cars travelling past outside I can enjoy the feeling of embarking on a journey of my own . . . a journey of relaxation and peace.' Acknowledging and positively utilizing noises in this way can allow them in time to fade into the background.

Sometimes, rather than outside noise disturbing you, it can be what is going on *in* your mind that is distracting. It can be unhelpful if during self-hypnosis all sorts of thoughts keep flying around in your head. If you wish to slow down your racing thoughts you may find the following approach useful. Stanton (1990) suggests picturing in your mind a luxurious black curtain. As thoughts enter your head allow them to drift across the curtain out through the other side of your mind. Then focus on the soft warm curtain once more.

(An extended version of this approach appears in chapter 6 for people suffering with insomnia.)

Find the symbolic imagery that works best for you. Be creative! For example, I once had a patient who came to see me for help regarding the problem of an overactive mind. At night, lying in bed, he could not sleep as his mind would not settle. He compared the feeling of racing thoughts in his head to a merry-go-round revolving at high speed. I explained how he could use symbolic imagery to calm his thoughts. From then on, whenever he wanted to help still his mind, all he did was imagine the merry-go-round, pull out the plug, and watch it gradually slow down until it stopped completely! He found this greatly helped to quieten his mind at the end of each day, allowing him to practise some self-hypnosis before drifting into a peaceful sleep.

## Different Ways to Give Suggestions

Some time was spent in chapter 3 examining the structuring of suggestions to ensure that they can work in the most positive way possible, both in and out of hypnosis. What we have not yet explored, however, is the notion of choice regarding the manner in which you can give yourself suggestions once practising self-hypnosis. Before learning to put yourself into a hypnotic state it is appropriate to give this area some consideration.

There are various ways you can give yourself suggestions when practising self-hypnosis. One way is to simply repeat your positive suggestions to yourself in your mind. However, some people find that in time, as they achieve deeper trance states, their conscious mind can become so relaxed and 'drifty' that it can be a bit of an effort to put in the suggestions! If you find this, you may prefer to write out your suggestions before you begin your self-hypnosis session. It is useful to read them over about ten times so that your mind is familiar with them. You can then pre-programme your subconscious mind to work with the suggestions during self-hypnosis by saying to yourself something like the following: 'As I do my self-hypnosis I want you, my subconscious mind, to reinforce these suggestions and help to make them become a reality for me in my life in an appropriate way.' Alternatively, the self-hypnosis session can be recorded from start to finish on a tape which can then be played each time you wish to practise self-hypnosis.

Whatever your depth of trance and whichever way you choose to relay positive messages to the deeper part of your mind, be reassured your time in hypnosis can be of considerable benefit to you. I would encourage you to experiment and find the approach that feels most comfortable and right for you.

## Exploring Your Imagination

It was Aristotle who stated, 'The soul never thinks without a picture.' The fact is, of course, that we have four other senses in addition to sight – hearing, smell, touch and taste. People can vary in the importance they place on each of these when taking in information about the world and using the senses in their imagination. Although most people will have moments when they use all the senses, the rest of the time they tend to be more attentive to only one or two of them. For example, artists are claimed to be very 'visual', while musicians are said to favour 'auditory' input.

To highlight the way you utilize your senses in your imagination, experiment with each of them as in *figure 4*. If you find some easier than others then more than likely you have identified your predominant senses. On the other hand, you may not experience any dramatic differences between your senses at all.

If some of your senses are weaker than others they can be trained with practice in self-hypnosis, helping to enrich that experience even further. Usually, leading from a predominant sense to a weaker one can help in this respect. For instance, if your sense of smell is weak in your imagination

| Visual (sight) | Auditory (hearing) | Kinesthetic (touch) |
|---|---|---|
| Imagine what your favourite room at home looks like. | Hear your favourite piece of music in your mind. | Imagine placing your hand under a tap of running water. |
| See in your mind the face of someone you love. | Imagine the sound of someone calling your name. | Feel in your mind the sensation of shaking hands with someone. |

| Olfactory (smell) | Gustatory (taste) |
|---|---|
| Breathe in the smell of freshly cut flowers in your mind. | Taste your favourite meal in your mind. |
| Imagine the smell of your favourite meal. | Feel that tangy taste as you imagine placing a segment of orange in your mouth. |

*Figure 4  Testing your senses in your imagination*

but you are very visual, it may help first to visualize your favourite meal. This can then 'lead' you to nurturing the sense of the smell of that meal in your mind. To improve the skill of using any sense in your imagination, practice is the key. Since a mental image can be worth literally hundreds of verbal suggestions, it is particularly beneficial to develop your visual sense.

## LEARNING HOW TO RELAX

The benefits of relaxation are many. Once people have learned how to relax they often report such changes as better sleeping habits and a general feeling of calm and ease in themselves. Achieving a relaxed body and state of mind is also a pleasant and beneficial way to begin self-hypnosis. It may be, therefore, that you will use the following technique prior to self-hypnosis, or else incorporate it into one of the inductions in the following section.

## Progressive Body Relaxation

It may be that you find it useful, for this and other exercises in the book, to record the structure of the exercise on a tape. It can help to use a soft voice tone and leave pauses where appropriate so that you can play the tape to guide yourself through your relaxation. Alternatively, you can ask someone to read the structure to you until you have become more familiar with what you are doing or have memorized the exercise. The word 'you' in the exercises may be substituted with the pronoun 'I' if appropriate. Use whatever feels most effective for you.

Progressive relaxation was developed by Dr Edmund Jacobson (1974) and is a very practical technique for releasing tension in your muscles. As the name suggests, it involves relaxing your body gradually in individual steps. Put aside a minimum of 20 minutes to really enjoy the following exercise.

### Exercise

1 Sit or lie down somewhere comfortable. Close your eyes.
2 Slowly tense the muscles of your feet and hold this tension for a moment. Now let the tension go very gradually.
3 Continue this flexing and relaxing, working upward through the muscle groups of the body – calves, thighs, buttocks, stomach, chest, back, hands, arms, shoulders, neck and face. As you work through the muscles you may wish to picture in your mind's eye each area easing out, seeing the muscles and tissues relaxing. Gently allow every muscle, every nerve and every fibre to let go.
4 Enjoy the sense of comfort and relaxation that follows.

45

# HYPNOTIC INDUCTIONS

As stated in chapter 1, to get the most from practising self-hypnosis it is vital to have a reasonable understanding of the subject. So before reading any further, ensure that you have read and are familiar with the preceding chapters.

Many hypnotic inductions are particularly suited to self-hypnosis. Three such induction techniques will be described here – the Eye Fixation Technique, the Relaxation Method, and the Staircase Induction. Once you have become accustomed to each of these techniques you can decide which one feels most comfortable to you, or indeed make up your own induction by combining techniques. Be creative with suggestions and imagery (see chapters 3 and 6). Give yourself about 20 to 30 minutes for each induction. Enjoy them!

## *The Eye Fixation Technique*

The aim of this technique is to induce the hypnotic state by helping to develop a sense of fatigue and heaviness in the eye muscles and eyelids. Repeated suggestions and the boredom generated from gazing at a spot for a long time are utilized in this respect. Although it is not necessary for the eyes to close most people find it more pleasant to allow this to happen in time.

### *Exercise*

1 Sit down and make yourself comfortable. Take a few deep breaths and look in front of you.
2 Locate a spot above your line of sight and stare at it.
3 Continue to focus all your attention on the spot. Keep your gaze fixed on it at all times. Often people can report visual distortions of the spot. For example, it may appear to move, become fuzzy or even disappear. Notice if you experience any such distortions with your spot.
4 It may be that as time passes, your eyelids begin to feel

heavy as you blink or stare, almost as if there were little weights attached to your eyelashes. Alternatively, you may just feel tired of staring at that spot and wish to close your eyes so that you can ease into a comfortable relaxed state. The harder you try to keep your eyes from closing the harder it can become not to close them. Regardless of how heavy your eyes are feeling, decide when it will be most comfortable for you to allow yourself the luxury of closing them.

5 All in your own way and in your own time you can notice that feeling of relaxation beginning to develop. Your breathing can slow down to a comfortable even pace as you allow this to happen. Enjoy that spread of comfort. Allow it to reach out and touch every part of you, right now or after your next few breaths. Throughout this induction, experiment with suggestions of your own in your mind to encourage relaxation and eye closure.

6 Now you can spend some time in this comfortable state, focusing on and working towards your goals of positive change.

7 Suggest to yourself that when you open your eyes you will feel refreshed, calm and alert. Count down from 3 to 1. Open your eyes.

## The Relaxation Method

The relaxation method incorporates relaxed breathing, suggestions of calm, and muscle relaxation to induce a peaceful trance state. Aim for a slow, even breathing pattern.

*Exercise*

1 Sit down and make yourself comfortable. Close your eyes.

2 Focus on your breathing. It can be interesting to notice all the different sensations as you breathe: the rise and fall of the ribcage, and the breath a little bit cooler as you breathe in, warmer as you breathe out.

47

3 Becoming absorbed in the gentle rhythm of your breathing in time can become quite soothing – like the feeling of being rocked in a cradle as a child or swaying on a swing. Allow that breath to slow down to a comfortable, even pace, all happening by itself in its own way and time.

4 As your breathing continues to become more comfortable, focus on the rest of yourself right now. Scan your body from top to toe for tensions of any kind, whether they be in your body or mind, consciously or even subconsciously lurking.

5 Wherever those tensions may be, allow them to leave your body as you exhale. As you breathe out more and more, they will become less and less. Enjoy that feeling of cleansing your body of tension in this very special way. As you inhale, your mind can give your body permission to breathe a sense of comfort and calm into your body.

6 Over time, as you breathe tensions out of your body and comfort and calm into your body, you can just allow your relaxation to deepen as you breathe into calmness and peace. Work through your body, focusing on the comfort of allowing the muscles to ease out more and more with each breath you take. Encourage the comfort you feel in the most comfortable part of you at this moment to sweep and spread gently throughout your body. (You could incorporate some progressive body relaxation work at this point if you so wished.)

7 Spend some time working on your positive goals of change, using imagery and suggestions as appropriate.

8 Suggest to yourself that when you open your eyes you will feel refreshed, calm and alert. Count down from 3 to 1. Open your eyes.

## The Staircase Induction

The following structure can be used as an induction in itself or incorporated into any other induction as a deepening technique. If for any reason you are not comfortable working with the image of a staircase in your mind, you do have other options with this type of induction. For example, you could use the image of a lift moving down through different floors in a building, or count your steps forward on a path leading down a hill in your mind. This will become clearer as you work through the following exercise.

*Exercise*

1 Sit down and make yourself comfortable. Close your eyes.

2 Imagine yourself at the top of a beautiful staircase. Examine it in detail in your mind. What is it made of? Does it have a banister or handrail? Is it indoors or outdoors?

3 This staircase can have steps leading down to the most comfortable and relaxing place you can imagine. Decide now in your mind what sort of a place this will be. For instance, you may choose a garden, a beach or a cosy room with a comfortable armchair by the fire. It could be a place you have been to before or one you create in your imagination. Make it every bit as beautiful as you would like it to be.

4 In a few moments, as you count yourself down these steps in your mind, you can become more relaxed and at ease with each step you take.

5 Count yourself down the steps from 1 to 20 in time with each or every second out breath (exhalation). This can have the effect of helping to slow and steady the breathing pattern even further.

6 Intersperse suggestions for relaxation throughout. For instance, 'As I continue my descent to this beautiful place, a feeling of deep calm can seep through to the very core of my being,' or 'When I reach the last step I can feel wonderfully relaxed and comfortable.'

7 Having reached the bottom of the staircase, you now find yourself in that special place you have chosen. Explore its beauty, using all your senses in your imagination. Firstly, you may wish to use your sense of sight by visualizing this place in detail in your mind. Then

**The Eye Fixation Technique**

Stare at a spot in front of you above eye level. Give suggestions for relaxation and eye closure. Work on your goals of positive change. Give the final suggestion for calmness and alertness before counting from 3 to 1 and opening your eyes.

**The Relaxation Method**

Close your eyes. Focus on your breathing. Allow all tensions to leave your body as you exhale. Breathe in a sense of calm and comfort with each inhalation. Encourage with appropriate suggestion the slowing down of the breathing and relaxation of the muscles of the body. Work on your goals of positive change. Give the final suggestion for calmness and alertness before counting from 3 to 1 and opening your eyes.

**The Staircase Induction**

Close your eyes. Imagine yourself at the top of a staircase with 20 steps leading to your special place of relaxation. As you count from 1 to 20 down the steps in time with your exhalations, allow a sense of relaxation to develop and deepen with each step you take. Explore your special place with all your senses in your imagination. Work on your goals of positive change. To come out, reverse the manner in which you entered hypnosis, counting back up the steps from 20 to 1 in time with your inhalations. Give the final suggestion for calmness and alertness before opening your eyes.

*Figure 5 Hypnotic inductions summary*

move through your other senses by smelling, touching, hearing and even tasting what surrounds you, if appropriate. Make everything as real as possible in your mind so that you can almost feel you are actually there.

8 Find somewhere comfortable to sit in this scene, a spot where you can work with the suggestions and imagery of your choice.

9 To come out of hypnosis simply reverse the way you came in. Count yourself back up the steps from 20 to 1, this time counting on each or every second in breath (inhalation). This will help you to become progressively more alert as you approach the top of the staircase in your mind.

10 Suggest that when you open your eyes you can feel refreshed, calm and alert. Open your eyes. Have a nice stretch!

During the preceding exercises you may have experienced subtle or even dramatic physical and psychological changes. For instance, you may have become aware of feelings of heaviness, lightness, warmth, tingling sensations or numbness. You may also have found that you became completely absorbed in feelings of relaxation. Perhaps you even experienced some time distortion whereby you thought your time in hypnosis longer or shorter than it actually was. All these are common and perfectly normal experiences of the hypnotic state. However, it does not need to become a matter of concern if you did not experience any of the above. As previously stated, each person experiences hypnosis in their own personal way. What is of prime importance is that you have taken some time to relax and work positively on yourself to your benefit.

Particularly to begin with, it is important to keep your self-hypnosis routine predictable and simple. Be flexible. Create your own self-hypnosis induction that works best for you. Then, with practice, it can become easier to drift into a deeply comfortable hypnotic state. As Napoleon said: 'Victory belongs to the most persevering.'

# 6

# Practical Therapy for a Range of Problems

The more you connect to the power within you, the more you
can be free in all areas of your life.

Louise L Hay

THE AIM OF THIS CHAPTER is to outline some introductory
concepts for therapy in a range of different areas. You
can experiment with these ideas either in self-hypnosis or
in addition to such work, as appropriate. We will be focusing on the following topics: habit disorders, anxiety, fears
and phobias, confidence and self-esteem, sexual problems,
pain control and medical conditions. Regardless of what you
wish to work on, it may be appropriate to read through all
these sections since most of the techniques and approaches
discussed are flexible and can be applied to many areas. You
will notice that certain simple techniques, such as the 'stop'
technique and 'mental rehearsal', are recommended time
and time again because of their universal benefit.

## HABIT DISORDERS

This section will deal in detail with the habit disorders of
smoking and overeating since they are the most common
reasons for individuals seeking help.

### Smoking

In a survey conducted by Dr Keith Hearne (1994), smokers
were asked what they would do if given an ultimatum to

choose between their spouse and smoking. All females reported they would give up smoking, but one in six males claimed they would give up their wives! These men obviously wish to remain smokers and therefore would not benefit from hypnotherapy or indeed any approach to help them become non-smokers! Also, for people who feel they *should* stop smoking but who do not really want to give up, therapy will be unsuccessful. For self-hypnosis to help you become a non-smoker it is of vital importance that you really want to stop smoking. Be honest with yourself. As we have already said, you cannot make anyone do something they do not want to do using hypnosis.

If you are internally motivated and determined to become a non-smoker this will be reinforced even further if at the outset you make a list of the benefits you will obtain from being a non-smoker. For example, people often include in such a list that they will:

- feel healthier
- smell fresher and feel cleaner
- feel fitter
- have extra money
- feel more in control and proud of their achievement

It will also be important, as discussed in chapter 4, for you to address any possible underlying reasons and secondary gains of the habit at this point.

Usually, habits seem to occur 'automatically' without conscious involvement. To make a conscious decision to stop a habit it can first of all be necessary to become consciously aware of the behaviour it involves. It is useful to ask yourself the following questions: 'When do I smoke most? When do I smoke least?' Perhaps you have wanted to become a non-smoker for some time now. Maybe you have even made some attempts to quit smoking in the past. What has stopped you from changing so far? When exploring your habit, it can also be productive to imagine a smoking situation in your mind and identify the thoughts and feelings you are usually experiencing prior to having a cigarette. If you feel it would provide even more insight, you could take this step further by monitoring each occasion you actually smoke, using a structure such as that shown in *figure* 6, p. 56.

Once the thoughts and feelings underlying and maintaining your habit are unearthed, many of the ideas presented in chapter 3 of this book can be of use. For example, you can use the 'stop' technique to combat negative thinking patterns. In self-hypnosis you can, for instance, give yourself suggestions for feeling calmer, stronger, more confident and in control, emphasizing to your subconscious mind the benefits of being a non-smoker. Times when you used to smoke can be turned into post-hypnotic cues for healthier activities, like taking a walk or taking a few deep breaths leading to a more relaxed feeling. Some people also find it useful to have cue cards with positive suggestions such as 'I am becoming healthier' stuck to their mirror, desk, in the car, and so on.

The technique in the exercise that follows is known as the 'swish'. It can be utilized with a range of different areas, including the habit of smoking. Created by Bandler (1985), it makes use of imagery to help combat the effect of any past, confusing messages your subconscious mind has received regarding your habit and what you truly want for yourself. The technique achieves this by further clarifying for the deeper part of your mind what you want and what you do not want. The 'swish' also helps the process of reprogramming your predominant thoughts to move in a more positive direction. This is particularly useful as usually we tend to gravitate towards our predominant thoughts. When you direct your mind in this positive way, you will notice how often your feelings and behaviour will have a very strong tendency to go in the same direction. Be flexible and creative with

| Date | Time | Location and Activity | Thoughts | Feelings | Score |
|------|------|----------------------|----------|----------|-------|
| 10.9.94 | 10am | At work preparing for a meeting | 'I feel anxious about speaking in front of everyone.' | Stressed | 3 |
| | | | | | |

Craving score: 3 = I have to have one
2 = I fancy one
1 = I can do without one

*Figure 6 A possible structure for self-monitoring of the smoking habit*

the imagery, making it personal and appropriate to your situation.

*Exercise*

1 Close your eyes and allow yourself to become gently relaxed.
2 See a screen in your mind as if you are at the cinema. Now see on this screen an image of the way you *do not want to be*. For example, it could be a picture of you looking very unhealthy with a cigarette in your hand. It could also feature those you love in the background, looking concerned. Whatever picture you decide on, make it as unpleasant as can be. Experience the feelings that come with looking at that image.
3 Now wipe this 'negative' image away from the screen. Once you have done that, see on the screen an image of the way you *want to be*. Make it as pleasant and attractive as possible, incorporating into it all the benefits of being a non-smoker. For instance, it could be a picture of you and your loved ones looking fit and healthy on a special holiday paid for by the money you would have otherwise spent on cigarettes. Step into that image in your mind and stay there until you sense how good it feels. Enjoy and take time to explore these positive feelings before wiping that positive image off the screen, leaving it blank once more.
4 Now see the 'negative' picture big and bright on the screen. Put a small, dark image of the 'positive' picture in the lower right-hand corner, stuck on like a stamp in the wrong place on a postcard.
5 As fast as you can say the word 'swish', allow the small, dark positive image to grow big and bright, covering the negative image so that it becomes dim and shrinks away completely.
6 Once this 'swish' has been completed, blank the screen or, alternatively, open your eyes.
7 'Swish' the images in the way described about five times.

Each time see if you can do it that bit quicker. Be sure to blank the screen or open your eyes at the end of each 'swish'.

8 Before completing this exercise, imagine once more the 'negative' image in your mind. If the 'swish' has been effective this image should be hard to get, or at least less clear in your mind than it was before you did this technique. Notice how easily and clearly you can bring the positive image into your mind. This positive image can now be the predominant image in your mind.

9 If you have not obtained the desired result, do the 'swish' again. Figure out how you can make the imagery more appropriate or what else you can do to make it benefit you. Remember – be creative!

Imagery can be utilized in a range of other productive ways – for example, by rehearsing success at being a non-smoker in your mind before entering a threatening situation. To reduce cravings you can suggest to yourself the way you would prefer to feel by focusing on appropriate imagery in your mind to help bring about these more positive feelings. You may become a non-smoker after one session of self-hypnosis or it may take several weeks. Allow things to develop at your own pace. Once you become a non-smoker it will then be important to reinforce your work over a period of months to keep you determined and strong.

## Slimming

Being overweight can be the result of a range of different causes. Some people have learnt unhealthy eating habits when growing up, others may overeat because of emotional problems, and a very small number, for whom hypnotherapy will not be an appropriate means of management, can be overweight due to hormonal or other physical disorders. For many of you it will not be necessary to consult a doctor before embarking on a programme of weight loss. You may merely wish to lose a few pounds in order to feel healthier, fit into a new outfit, or look good on holiday. However, those of you wishing to lose several stone in weight would be well advised to seek medical advice first.

If you decide to visit your doctor, you can be checked out for any medical condition which could be causing obesity, for example, hypothyroidism or Cushings disease. A safe dietary regime can then be established and subsequent weight loss monitored. Some doctors advocate the use of appetite suppressant drugs such as diethylproprion and phentermine. However, the General Medical Council has suggested that these be avoided as they do not improve the long-term outcome. The medical profession as a body is also opposed to rigid diets for people who wish to lose weight, except in certain circumstances.

For the most part, healthy eating patterns are the key to success for slimmers. Such an approach is less drastic than dieting and allows the individual to maintain weight loss indefinitely. It is also less damaging on the body. Although it is beyond the scope of this book to look at the topic in any detail, it is appropriate to highlight a few points regarding nutrition. As a general rule your diet should contain an adequate amount of carbohydrate, protein, fat, vitamins, minerals, trace elements, roughage (fibre) and water. You will find the nutrient content of some common everyday foods in *figure 7*. Cut simple sugars (such as biscuits and chocolate) down to a bare minimum. Fats should be polyunsaturated, and cut animal fats out of your diet completely if possible. Increase your protein from vegetable sources (for instance, soya beans and pulses). Plan your day. Eat meals regularly and avoid snacking. Also note that weight loss is not just about what you eat. The calories you take in need to be burned off and the only way to increase this process is to exercise. With the help of your doctor, choose an activity that is both safe and enjoyable for you.

Many of you are probably already aware of what you should be doing! It may be, however, that you need a little help, particularly in the motivation department.

| Food | Nutrient Content | | | | | |
|---|---|---|---|---|---|---|
| | Carbo-hydrate | Protein | Fat | Water | Energy per 100g (3.5oz) | |
| | | | | | kj | kcal |
| Wholewheat flour | 3 | 2 | 1 | 2 | 1,420 | 339 |
| White bread | 3 | 1 | 1 | 2 | 1,020 | 243 |
| Butter | 1 | 1 | 3 | 2 | 3,320 | 793 |
| Milk (fresh, whole) | 1 | 1 | 1 | 3 | 276 | 66 |
| Cheese (cheddar) | 1 | 2 | 3 | 3 | 1,780 | 425 |
| Haddock (fried) | 1 | 2 | 1 | 3 | 733 | 175 |
| Beef steak (fried) | 0 | 2 | 2 | 3 | 1,140 | 273 |
| Rice (raw) | 3 | 1 | 1 | 2 | 1,510 | 361 |
| Potatoes | 2 | 1 | 1 | 3 | 293 | 70 |
| Peas (canned) | 2 | 1 | 1 | 3 | 360 | 86 |
| Cabbage (boiled) | 1 | 1 | 1 | 3 | 38 | 9 |
| White sugar | 3 | 1 | 0 | 1 | 1,650 | 394 |
| Apple | 2 | 1 | 1 | 3 | 197 | 47 |
| Orange (with peel) | 1 | 1 | 1 | 3 | 113 | 27 |
| Beer (bitter) | 1 | 1 | 1 | 3 | 130 | 31 |
| Spirits (70% proof) | 1 | 1 | 0 | 3 | 929 | 222 |

**Scores**  0 = No Content  1 = Low content
2 = Medium content  3 = High content

*Figure 7 Nutrient content of some common foods*

Self-hypnosis can be that help. Working on yourself can facilitate positive behavioural change and the subsequent adoption of healthier eating habits. It can also increase the likelihood of a long-term successful outcome.

Most of the suggestions and ideas given for those wishing to become non-smokers are also relevant to slimmers. If you have not read the previous section you may find it beneficial to do so. For instance, it is useful for increasing motivation to make a list of all the benefits you will obtain from being slimmer (see chapter 4 for an example of such a list for slimmers). Exploration of eating habits can help you to become more conscious of your eating patterns. This can allow you to identify the thoughts and feelings you are usually experiencing before you eat and thus clarify areas you may need to target with your work. It will also be important to address the area of possible underlying reasons and secondary gains (see chapter 4). The 'stop' technique, appropriate post-hypnotic suggestions and the 'swish' technique (see previous section) can all be of use, as can the utilization of suggestions and imagery to rehearse and reinforce in your mind that slimmer person you want to be.

Particularly if your weight-loss goal is substantial, you may wish to break down your main goal into smaller 'digestible' steps to work towards. For instance, you could have weekly and monthly targets. In general, a safe rate of weight loss is no more than two or three pounds per week. Be sure to reward yourself along the way for your achievements with non-food treats – a new outfit, a book, flowers, and so on. Use your self-hypnotic techniques frequently every day to keep you determined, motivated, in control and positive while the weight comes off, and stays off.

A lot of overweight individuals find they are prompted to eat in response to a range of different cues other than hunger. Indeed, such people have often lost touch with their body's needs and what it feels like to be hungry. If you feel you are such a person, the following strategy will help you to listen to and be more in tune with your body's food requirements. Andreas and Andreas (1989) created this method from their study of how naturally thin people think about and respond to food. Practise it in your mind to prepare you in advance for a range of different situations. For example, you may like to do this exercise before lunch or before going to a party.

*Exercise*

1 Close your eyes and allow yourself to become gently relaxed.
2 Explore in your mind the various triggers that can act as a signal for you to eat. For instance, is it the time of day, the sight of food, a thought about food, the feeling of hunger or some other feeling?
3 Check how your stomach feels at this moment and ask yourself what would feel good in your stomach. Visualize a possible choice of food.
4 Imagine eating the food you have chosen and get a sense of how it will feel in your stomach over the time to follow.
5 Compare this feeling over time with how your stomach would feel if you ate nothing at this point. Only if it feels better will you keep this food as a possibility for consumption.
6 Test out as many other possible food options as you wish until you have decided on what would make your stomach feel most comfortable over time. (Usually, fattening and unhealthy foods do not feel good in the stomach as time passes by and can often leave people feeling sluggish and tired.)
7 Once you have finished this exercise, eat in reality the food of your choice that will allow the best feeling in your stomach over time.

This exercise can also be used to help you decide, when in the middle of eating something, on the appropriate time to finish. You can, for example, ask yourself, 'Will my stomach feel more or less comfortable over time if I have this next bite?' Getting into the habit of using the above strategy can lead to a gradual, healthy weight loss and, subsequently, the maintenance of your positive results.

Hypnotherapy can be an effective intervention for smoking and overeating. Whether you wish to become a non-smoker or be slimmer, or both, self-hypnosis is a powerful, therapeutic ability which can help you to adjust your thoughts, attitudes and behaviour accordingly. No one technique will be effective for everyone, so be sure to experiment to find what works best for you.

## ANXIETY, FEARS AND PHOBIAS

A certain amount of anxiety in life can be helpful, motivating us to deal with the problems underlying our tensions. However, being over-anxious can adversely affect health and happiness. For some people, levels of high anxiety can be persistent enough to induce symptoms such as chronic muscular tension, self-perpetuating hyperactivity, excessive worry and apprehensive expectation.

For others this anxiety can develop that bit further, into a deep fear or panic. Such people can often suffer from phobias. The word 'phobia' comes from the Greek word 'phobos' and means 'panic fear'. A phobia can be defined as an excessive, unrealistic, uncontrollable fear which is triggered off by a particular object, activity or situation. It differs from ordinary fear in that it is persistent over a long period of time, irrational and involves avoidance of the trigger.

Many doctors recommend the use of psychotherapeutic techniques, including self-hypnosis, in the management of anxiety, fears and phobias. With the introduction of the benzodiazepine group of drugs (for example, diazepam, lorazepam and temazepam) a few decades ago, it was felt that anxiety and other related disorders could be managed with these anxiolytic drugs. However, these drugs have an addictive potential and are mainly used nowadays for short-term management. Generally, they will not improve the long-term outcome for the anxiety sufferer.

Self-management of the manifestations of anxiety is worth considering when your problem is not too severe or if you just wish to see how much you can improve things on your own. It is beneficial at the outset to make a list of all the ways in which your life will be better when you have conquered anxiety and fear. Reading this list frequently will keep you encouraged and motivated. Your work may also involve tackling possible root causes and addressing any secondary gains, see chapter 4 .

If anxiety is preventing you living your life as you would wish, chances are you could be talking negatively to yourself in your thoughts. The 'stop' technique and the utilization of suggestions and imagery to rehearse and reinforce the way you want to be will be very beneficial in this respect (see chapter 3). Since it is impossible for someone to be relaxed and anxious at the same time, employing the 'progressive relaxation' exercise outlined in chapter 5 will also be appropriate.

The most important aspect of treatment of fear is exposure to that fear. Depending on the level of your anxiety or fear it may be advisable to work with a trained therapist through the following exercise. It is a standard technique for use with fears and phobias and involves a gradual step-by-step approach. Work through the exercise over the coming weeks and months.

*Exercise*

1 Construct a target ladder of ten rungs, ranging from a step producing the least anxiety up to the step producing the most. For example, if you are suffering from agoraphobia involving a fear of being trapped, are unable to get help,

and have become housebound as a result of this fear, it may be that you construct a ladder similar to the following.

1 Putting on a coat in preparation for going outside.
2 Standing at the front door.
3 Taking a few steps away from the front door while a friend is with me.
4 Taking a few steps away from the front door alone.
5 Walking down to a small local shop and back with a friend.
6 Walking down to a small local shop and back alone.
7 Travelling a longer distance to larger shops with a friend.
8 Travelling a longer distance to larger shops alone.
9 Staying in a crowded shopping centre for 5 minutes with a friend.
10 Staying in a crowded shopping centre for 5 minutes alone.

2 Only when comfortably relaxed, practise in your imagination the first step of your ladder. See it and experience it in your mind in as much detail as possible. Use positive suggestions and imagery to make it the very best way it can be. If you become anxious at any point, abandon the scene in your mind temporarily and focus on allowing your breath to become calmer and relaxed once more before returning to the step.

3 Then, only when you feel comfortable in your imagination with that step, carry it out in reality. (It is preferable to do this immediately after your relaxation session if possible.)

4 Practise your first step in reality until you feel confident to move on to the second step, and then work in the same way.

5 Progress up the ladder at your own pace, always ensuring that you are comfortable with the step in your imagination before carrying it out in reality. There is a temptation to want to move ahead too quickly – resist it!

6 After you have completed each step, reward yourself in some way.

No one can be in control all the time and escape anxious feelings. So, rather than expecting to abolish anxiety completely, aim at keeping it under control at a reasonable, healthy level. Accept and work in a positive way on your bad days. Celebrate the good ones, which can increase with time.

## CONFIDENCE AND SELF-ESTEEM

Nearly everyone from time to time experiences feelings of self-doubt. Many of us are inclined to be self-critical, focusing more on the negative than the positive aspects of ourselves. If you allow your thoughts regarding your worth and abilities to be negative, this will lead to negative feelings, attitudes and beliefs about yourself.

It makes sense, therefore, to support yourself in a positive way in your thoughts. Be your own best friend. Decide to speak to yourself in your mind in the same respectful and helpful way you would speak to others. It is important to offer yourself praise and motivation in all that you do. To develop confidence you will need to accept, understand and be kind to yourself. Becoming more confident is not about becoming egotistical or feeling you are better than those around you. It is about feeling good about yourself.

Usually, when working on confidence it is appropriate to isolate particular areas in your life where you wish to be more confident, and work on each of these in turn. For example, if you lack confidence regarding a prospective driving test you could work on this area with mental rehearsal, as outlined in chapter 3. This will help you to demonstrate your driving skills to the best of your ability without interference from excess nervousness. If you feel your self-esteem easily eroded by negative comments aimed at you by others, it is possible, for instance, to imagine having a protective guard around you which repels negativity, allowing only positive and constructive messages to flow through. Prioritize the areas you feel you need most help with and set to work with clear, realistic and achievable goals (see chapter 4).

The following technique adapted from the work of Stein (1963) employs hypnotic conditioning to give a useful method for increasing confidence when you feel you most need it. It is a flexible technique and as well as being of use when dealing with feelings of low confidence or self-esteem it can also be used for coping with negative emotions such as anxiety and anger.

*Exercise*

1 Close your eyes and allow yourself gently to relax.
2 Scan your memories and identify any time in your life when you felt confident.
3 Allow yourself to travel back to that experience. Re-live it in your mind and get a sense of those feelings you felt then. Explore and enjoy that positive time once more in your mind.
4 When you can experience that confident feeling, close your dominant hand into a tight fist. As you do this, allow those feelings of confidence to increase. That fist can represent your inner determination to be that more confident person.
5 As you clench your fist tighter still, allow that feeling of confidence to reach out and touch every part of you. The deeper part of your mind can memorize this marvellous feeling.
6 Repeatedly give yourself the post-hypnotic suggestion that, in future, whenever you close your dominant hand into a tight fist in this way you can once more enjoy this feeling of confidence. You can also suggest that you can be pleasantly surprised at how long afterwards this positive feeling can remain with you.
7 Relax and open that fist, allowing yourself to drift into an even more comfortable state.
8 Before completing your exercise, make that hand into a

tight fist of confidence again and notice how once more that positive memory and that confident feeling can come flowing through.

The more you practise this exercise, the stronger that association between clenching your fist and feeling confident can become. *Knowing* there is something you can do to increase your feeling of confidence in any situation can in itself increase your confidence still further. Learn to understand and build on your strengths and abilities. None of us is perfect, but we can strive to be the very best we can be.

## SEXUAL PROBLEMS

Sexual dysfunction involves disruption of the physiological mechanisms involved in one or more of the sexual response phases – sexual desire, arousal and orgasm. Although many sexual problems can be psychologically based, it would be wise to visit your doctor to rule out physical factors before working on this area with self-hypnosis. It will then be appropriate, either by yourself or with the help of a trained therapist, to give attention to the exploration of past sexual experiences and possible underlying reasons and secondary gains of the present problem (see chapter 4). If you are in a relationship it may be important to place it under careful scrutiny, since a dysfunction can in some cases have a couple-based cause. For example, Lipiccolo and Hogan (1979) state how a dysfunction can sometimes be 'a means of avoiding intimacy, of expressing hostility, of maintaining control in the relationship, or of retaliating for other grievances in the relationship'.

Araoz (1988) has the opinion that by the time we have reached adulthood we are often responding to many 'post-hypnotic suggestions' regarding sex. He notes that these suggestions have been given by parents, religion, society, the media and advertising. If these suggestions have been negative, sexual dysfunction can arise and much remedial work through positive everyday thoughts and suggestions in self-hypnosis may be required to combat myths and misinformation. Positive messages can also be conveyed to the subconscious mind when you mentally rehearse success and enjoyment in your sexual encounters. Because anxiety and stress can interfere with sexual responsiveness, learning to relax is also beneficial (see chapter 5).

The following technique draws from the ideas of Hammond (1990). Since inhibited sexual desire appears to be the most common sexual dysfunction (Kaplan, 1979), we will be focusing on this problem in the following exercise. However, due to the flexibility of the technique it can also be adapted for use with other sexual problems, including ejaculatory inhibition, orgasmic dysfunction and erectile dysfunction. It will be most appropriate to practise this exercise prior to anticipated lovemaking.

*Exercise*

1 Close your eyes and allow yourself to enter a peaceful self-hypnotic state.
2 Imagine entering a very special room which is situated in the part of your brain containing the controls for all your emotions and desires. (This part of the brain is known as the 'hypothalamus'.)
3 Notice in this room, for example, panels of different coloured lights and the sounds of the computers. Move to the panel of light which regulates your level of sexual desire.
4 On this panel of light there is a dial which can be set from 0 to 10. The number 10 represents a very high level of sexual desire. Notice which number this dial is set at presently.
5 Reach out in your mind and move that dial slowly up to the next number. As you do this, be aware of something altering inside you. It may be that you become conscious of a slight increase in sexual desire. Alternatively, that change in your desire may be so subtle to begin with that it may only register at a subconscious level.

6 You can further help those increases in sexual desire by engaging in sexual fantasies or dwelling on a personal sexual experience you really enjoyed. It can also be useful to use imagery in a symbolic way. For instance, as suggested by Godefroy (1992), you could give sexual energy a discernible form in your imagination, perhaps as a waterfall or a ray of light. Then, in your mind, see the form you have decided on surging through your body and eventually filling the abdomen. Allow this energy to flood that part of your body. Be creative in this work!

7 Take your time moving up through the numbers on the dial. Move at your own pace, only moving the dial to a new number when it feels right to do so.

8 Complete the exercise when you have reached a level of sexual desire that you feel happy with.

## PAIN CONTROL

It is possible to interrupt pain at various sites along its pathway through the body and brain (see *figure* 8). However, because pain serves the vital function of alerting us when something requires attention, it is not appropriate to switch it off without knowing why it is there. Pain can be classified into three types.

1 *Nocicepture pain.* This is pain caused by a noxious stimulus. It would include pain from an inflamed area of the body.

2 *Neurogenic pain.* This is pain due to an abnormal propagation of an impulse along the nerve (for example, peripheral neuropathy in a diabetic patient or reflex sympathetic dystrophy syndrome).

3 *Psychogenic pain.* This is mind-generated pain.

Before taking on board any programme of hypnotic pain control, it is important to see your doctor to ensure that the nature of the pain is understood and appropriate measures are taken to treat any obvious or underlying cause. It is safe

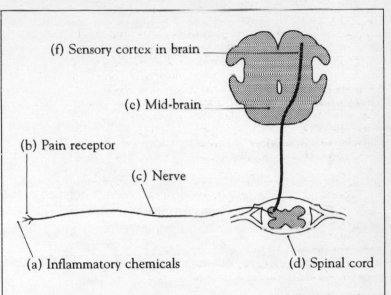

(f) Sensory cortex in brain

(e) Mid-brain

(b) Pain receptor

(c) Nerve

(a) Inflammatory chemicals          (d) Spinal cord

(a) by inhibiting the release of inflammatory chemicals and their action on pain receptors (for example, with aspirin or other non-steroidal anti-inflammatory drugs, and steroids themselves)

(b) by blocking the movement of ions across the membrane (for example, with local anaesthetic drugs)

(c) by blocking nerve transmission (for example, with local anaesthetic drugs)

(d) by using, for example, epidural or spinal anaesthetics, morphine or other opioid drugs, and acupuncture

(e) and (f) by using, for example, hypnosis, morphine and acupuncture

*Figure 8 How pain can be interrupted at various sites (a – f)*

to utilize hypnotic treatment in the alleviation of pain in the following circumstances:

1 in conjunction with medical treatment,
2 if medical diagnosis has shown that the pain is psychogenic, and
3 if the condition is not treatable medically.

When using self-hypnosis for pain control it is often advisable to leave a residual feeling so that injury, new symptoms or deterioration of your condition can be perceived and appropriately addressed.

Pain is not merely the perception of sensations of discomfort in isolation. It also includes a cognitive and emotional reaction to such sensations. Negative thoughts about pain, and the subsequent increase in anxiety and tension, can cause discomfort to be felt more intensely. It is therefore of paramount importance to work with your thoughts in a positive way for comfort (see chapter 3). Rather than continuously commenting on how bad your pain is, which only serves to reinforce discomfort, you could for instance speak to yourself in the following way: 'With each moment that passes I can feel that bit more comfortable and at ease.' Employing relaxation procedures will also be of benefit (see chapter 5). Additionally, it may be appropriate to address the possible presence of secondary gain (see chapter 4). This can be particularly relevant in cases of chronic intractable pain.

Various examples of how imagery can be utilized to ease discomfort have already been outlined in chapter 3. Re-read this section if you feel you need to refresh your memory. Analgesia, or dulling of pain, is often brought about by employing imagery and suggestions promoting numbness. For example, you could imagine you have received an injection of a powerful painkiller. Alternatively, you could give suggestions for numbness in one hand, encouraging it to feel as if it has 'gone to sleep' or is surrounded by ice. Once you have achieved the easier step of numbing your hand you can then place it on the affected area and give suggestions for the transfer of that numbness. Imagery can be further used as a distraction by allowing the mind to focus on imagery incompatible with the experience of pain. For instance, you may imagine taking a favourite countryside walk. The more you become absorbed in such imagery, the more your attention can be diverted from feelings of discomfort.

Usually it is easiest to work on pain at a stage when it is not too intense. However, there may be times when your pain is at a high level and you wish to practise self-hypnosis. If this is the case, attempting to block out the pain may prove difficult. Strange as it may sound, it will often be more beneficial to use the discomfort itself as the focus of your concentration rather than anything else. The following exercise is an example of how you might do this. It incorporates an adapted version of the work of Godefroy (1992). You will note that, as in the exercise in the previous section, a dial is utilized to help initiate and measure change.

*Exercise*

1 Close your eyes and allow yourself to enter a peaceful self-hypnotic state.
2 Explore your level of discomfort and rate it on an imaginary dial with numbers from 0 to 10, where 10 represents the most pain you ever experience. Set the dial at the number showing where you are with your discomfort at this moment.
3 Imagine your pain in the shape of a tunnel. As you enter the tunnel notice how the pain slightly intensifies. Allow this to be reflected in the movement of the dial.
4 Just as you have the power to increase your pain, so too can you decrease it. Walking through the tunnel you become aware of a pin-point of light in the distance. Each step you take brings you closer to that light and can increase your comfort and allow the number on your discomfort dial to move down at an appropriate pace. The

number you see on the dial can be the level of discomfort you feel.

5 Allow that circle of light at the end of the tunnel to become bigger and brighter as you approach it. As this happens notice how you become more and more comfortable.

6 You can determine how long or short this tunnel is. It will very much depend on your level of discomfort as you work through your pain.

7 When the discomfort dial has reached an acceptable level for you (perhaps the number 3 or 2), you can walk out of the tunnel in your mind, feeling more at ease and comfortable.

8 Take some time to reinforce these positive feelings in whatever way feels most appropriate to you before opening your eyes.

When treating pain with self-hypnosis it is important to be realistic regarding what you can achieve. You may notice improvement after one session. However, it is more usual that benefits will become more obvious with practice. It may be that you will require a session every day, or even twice daily to begin with. Motivation and the benefits of controlling the pain will generally be important in determining success. But if you are prepared to put in the effort, the results with self-hypnosis can be very rewarding. Gargiulo (1983) found that subjects receiving hypnotic skills training, when compared with those who did not learn such skills, showed an increase in tolerance of pain. They were also experiencing a greater reduction in levels of discomfort and seemed generally more positive in how they coped with their pain.

## MEDICAL CONDITIONS

There are many medical disorders that can benefit from the use of hypnosis. This is particularly true of those which have a significant psychosomatic element. However, please note that it is always wise to consult your doctor before embarking on any self-help programme in this area. In this section we will discuss the use of self-hypnosis with the following conditions: insomnia, premenstrual syndrome, eczema, asthma, high blood pressure, irritable bowel syndrome and cancer.

## Insomnia

As noted earlier, the word 'hypnosis' is derived from the Greek word 'hypnos' meaning sleep. It is now known that hypnosis and sleep are not the same state. However, practising self-hypnosis can be very helpful when wanting to ease into a peaceful sleep. In fact many of my patients often report that they find it difficult to get any work done on themselves in the hypnotic state if they are lying in bed. They nearly always fall asleep! This is why I usually recommend that you avoid lying down when doing self-hypnosis, unless you are actually working on insomnia.

A small percentage of sleeping difficulties can be as a result of physical disturbances such as depressive illness or pain. It may therefore be advisable to visit your doctor before embarking on a programme of self-hypnosis, particularly if sleep disturbance is associated with any physical symptoms. More common reasons for problems with sleeping are those which stem from anxiety and an overactive mind at bedtime. At night, self-hypnosis can help promote relaxation and distraction from adverse mental activities immediately prior to sleep. As outlined in chapter 5 when discussing how to deal with distractions, racing thoughts can be slowed down through the manipulation of symbolic imagery in a positive way.

Practising self-hypnosis during the day can be beneficial for the setting up of appropriate post-hypnotic suggestions for sleep. For instance, you could suggest the following to yourself: 'As I undress for bed I can notice how sleepy I become.' It is also useful to give yourself appropriate positive suggestions in your everyday thoughts. Negative thoughts such as 'If I do not sleep tonight I will be exhausted in the morning' only serve to create a fear of insomnia and reinforce the problem.

Mentally rehearsing in your imagination the way you want your night's sleep to be can also be beneficial. For instance, see yourself in your mind starting to feel relaxed as you turn off the light. When your head touches the pillow notice how comfortable your bed feels and enjoy that feeling of drifting into a comfortable, peaceful sleep. If you need to answer a 'call of nature' during the night, visualize yourself in your imagination slipping into sleep with ease once more when you return to bed. See yourself then waking in the morning feeling refreshed, rested and ready to face a brand-new day.

Just as it is important not to 'try' to make things happen when wishing to enter the hypnotic state (see chapter 1), it is equally important to keep conscious effort to a minimum at the time you want to drift into a state of sleep. The following exercise has been adapted from the ideas of Stanton (1990) and is designed for use at bedtime. It incorporates the staircase induction outlined in chapter 5. Let go when it feels right to do so and allow sleep to approach at its own pace. Sweet dreams!

*Exercise*

1 Close your eyes and allow yourself to enter a peaceful self-hypnotic state.
2 Imagine in your mind a luxurious black curtain. As thoughts enter your head, allow them to drift across the curtain and out through the other side of your mind. Then focus on the soft warm curtain once more.
3 Visualize yourself on a patio overlooking the most beautiful garden you have ever seen. Ten steps lead down to that garden.
4 In a few moments, as you count yourself down these steps

in your mind, you can become more relaxed and at ease with each step you take.

5 Count yourself down the steps from 1 to 10 in time with each or every second out breath (exhalation). Intersperse suggestions for relaxation throughout.

6 On reaching the bottom of the steps notice how calm and peaceful you feel. In your imagination explore the garden with all your senses. For example, perhaps you can see the different colours of the flowers as you breathe in their fragrance, feel the warmth of the sun on your face, hear birds singing in the trees or the odd bee humming from flower to flower in the distance.

7 Allow yourself to lie down on the soft grass, gazing up at the sky. Perhaps you can see wispy clouds drifting there. Maybe you can hear the whispering of the leaves rustling in the gentle breeze. As you notice some of these leaves dropping off the trees this can remind your mind that now is the time to let go.

8 As you enjoy the tranquillity of this place, allow yourself to ease into a comfortable and restful sleep.

### Premenstrual Syndrome (PMS)

When discussing the subject of PMS, both physical and emotional aspects need to be addressed. On a physical level there may be swelling and tenderness of the breasts, a bloated abdominal sensation with distension and abdominal cramps. The emotional aspects can include anger, tearfulness, emotional instability, depression, anxiety, diminished self-esteem and, in severe cases, suicidal tendencies. A range of treatments is available, with varying degrees of success. These include hormone therapy (similar to the oral contraceptive pill), vitamins such as pyridoxine (vitamin $B_6$) and evening primrose oil.

Self-hypnosis has been successfully used in the management of PMS even where other treatments have failed. Patients can gain much benefit from this approach. For ideas on how you may improve physical symptoms of discomfort please refer to the section in this chapter on pain control. With reference to working on emotional aspects, you may find it useful to re-read and follow the suggestions for tackling feelings of anxiety and low self-esteem in this chapter. Additionally, you may wish to practise the following exercise adapted from the work of Walch (1976). It can be particularly useful for dealing with negative emotions such as depression and anger.

*Exercise*

1 Close your eyes and allow yourself gently to relax.
2 Imagine that you are strolling down a beautiful country lane. Allow your relaxation to develop and increase with each step you take.
3 Enjoy and take interest in your surroundings by exploring them with all your senses in your mind. Make them every bit as beautiful as you would like them to be.
4 Imagine that you are carrying a large pack on your back. As the lane leads you up a small hill, notice the dead weight of this pack. The heavy contents of the pack can represent unwanted negative feelings.
5 On reaching the top of the hill you find an open gate leading into a beautiful meadow. In the middle sits a large, colourful, hot air balloon with a big basket beneath it. Large ropes hold the balloon down.
6 Walk over to the balloon and drop your heavy backpack to the ground. Open the pack and one by one take out its contents (representing those unwanted feelings) and place them in the basket. Notice how your negative feelings decrease more and more with each object you put into the basket. Enjoy that process.
7 As soon as you have disposed of the last object from the pack you can become aware of a feeling of deep relief and peace inside.
8 Nearby on the grass you may notice a large knife or hatchet. Use this to cut the ropes and set the balloon and basket free.

9 Lie down on the comfortable, warm, soft grass and
watch that balloon float away. As you do so, you
can notice a feeling of further release and calm. As
the balloon drifts further and further away, soon to be
out of view, really enjoy that feeling of being free from
those unwanted feelings.

10 Before completing this exercise, reinforce that new,
good feeling in your own way.

## Eczema

Eczema is an itchy inflammation of the skin. The condition
usually presents itself as scaly and red. When scratched, the
affected skin is prone to 'weeping' and can become very
uncomfortable and sore. There is often loss of sleep due to
this discomfort.

Although the exact cause of eczema is not known, it
seems that a higher incidence of the condition is found in
atopic individuals (those with a history of allergy), and its
immunological basis is quite similar to allergic asthma. It
also appears that stress and emotional disturbance can aggravate this disorder. It may therefore be important to address
any possible underlying influences promoting the condition
before dealing directly with the alleviation of eczema symptoms. For example, there are many ideas in this book on
how to help yourself to become a more relaxed person. You
may wish to employ the 'stop' technique with your everyday
thoughts and utilize suggestions and imagery in self-hypnosis
to rehearse and reinforce the calmer person you wish to be
(see chapter 3). Additionally, it may be that you engage in
'progressive relaxation' work as outlined in chapter 5.

The symptoms of itching and irritation associated with
eczema may be addressed in self-hypnosis as follows. Symbolic imagery (see chapter 3) can be used by first of all
visualizing an image that represents the discomfort. If, say,
the irritation feels like insects crawling over your skin, see
these insects in your mind. Then imagine, for example,

cool refreshing water flowing over your skin, washing away the insects and relieving and comforting the affected area. Pick imagery that will work best and be most soothing to you. Post-hypnotic suggestions can then be utilized to help reduce rubbing, picking and scratching. For instance, you may give yourself suggestions such as: 'Whenever I sense that irritation on my skin, I can remember the cool and comforting feeling of water,' or 'As my fingers touch my skin, even if this is at night while I sleep, I can become aware of this at some level of my mind and move my hand away from the affected area.'

The following exercise is an adaptation of suggestions formulated by Hammond (1990) to help reduce dermatologic irritation.

*Exercise*

1 Close your eyes and allow yourself to enter a peaceful self-hypnotic state.
2 Imagine a cooling ointment being spread on the affected areas of skin. This ointment is special and can promote rapid comfort and healing.
3 As you enjoy that soothing feeling, notice in your mind the skin changing, becoming softer and more normal in colour and appearance. Imagine the improved flow of blood through the skin, providing extra nourishment to aid this process of rapid healing.
4 Allow more and more of that ointment to be gently spread on the skin. Watch and feel it sink in.
5 Continue to repeat the preceding step until your skin is feeling comfortable and relieved.
6 Before completing this work, suggest that the comfort can remain with you until you once again take time to engage in the practice of this exercise.

*Asthma*

It is appropriate to use self-hypnosis with asthma in conjunction with medical management, including the use of

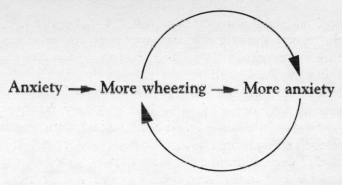

*Figure 9 The vicious circle caused by anxiety in an asthma attack*

bronchodilator inhalers, steroid inhalers and antibiotics. Asthma can involve the experience of symptoms such as shortness of breath, wheezing, coughing and tightness in the chest. These may be precipitated by a variety of different agents. In some instances it can be a life-threatening condition.

Asthma is affected by exercise, allergies and infections. In addition, research suggests (for example, French and Alexander, 1941) that an emotional component may often operate, aggravating, and even in some cases bringing about, asthma symptoms. With this in mind it can be appropriate to investigate precipitating factors of the disorder and to use self-hypnosis to help unblock and release negative feelings. The exercise involving the hot air balloon outlined in the section on premenstrual syndrome may prove beneficial in this respect.

Self-hypnosis for asthma is essentially a preventive treatment. For example, asthmatics are usually in a position to detect the beginning of an attack, and with this can come anxiety and anticipatory fear of not being able to catch their breath. This can powerfully aggravate the development of an attack, forming a vicious circle as shown in *figure 9*.

Linking appropriate post-hypnotic suggestions for relaxation to the signal or precursor of attacks and keeping your everyday thoughts working in a calming way can often help to prevent an attack. It may also be beneficial to rehearse potentially stressful situations in your mind in advance, seeing yourself coping in a relaxed way, breathing freely and comfortably.

Although the bulk of the work with asthma is carried out prior to prospective attacks, there are ways to ease the situation once an attack has already started. In order to help you be creative and use imagery and suggestion in the most beneficial way possible, it is appropriate to look briefly at the pathophysiology of asthma. When the offending agent brings on an attack of asthma, the diameter of the airway in the lung is reduced. There then follows an obstruction to airflow, particularly expiration. Three factors are responsible for this reduction in airway size.

1 Bronchoconstriction – the bronchi (or airways in the lungs) become constricted (narrowed).
2 Hypersecretion of mucus – the cells lining the airways produce an excessive amount of mucus and form mucous plugs.
3 Mucosal oedema – the cells lining the airway become swollen.

The following exercise includes imagery and suggestions originating from an understanding of what is happening physically at the beginning of and during an asthma attack. It also borrows some useful ideas from the work of Gibbons (1979) in this area.

*Exercise*

1 If you feel an attack coming on, or even if it has already begun, close your eyes and, experimenting with what works best for you, gently work at calming yourself.
2 Start counting up to 50 slowly in your mind.
3 Before each count take a deep breath in and clench your fists.
4 On each count let that breath go, repeating the word

'calm' to yourself. Unclench your fists, opening your hands wide. Allow this to represent your throat and airway opening up as the muscle in the walls of the bronchi relaxes more and more. Encourage your body to release as much tension as possible.

5 Bring in suggestions and imagery of your choice. For example:

- Imagine a miniature fireman standing in the centre of your airway. Visualize him hosing down the wall of your bronchi, loosening and clearing away the mucous plugs, calming inflammation and reducing swelling. As you see this in your mind, feel your chest expanding more and more.

- Imagine an Olympic runner in a race. Your breathing is matching his as he runs over the finishing line and wins. As he slows down to a comfortable jog and finally a walk, notice how the breathing of this fit athlete becomes slower and easier. Allow your breathing to slow down similarly and become even, as your lung and chest muscles relax more and more.

6 Complete the exercise once counting is terminated and breathing is back to normal. Visualize cool, clean air rushing freely down the airways that you have opened up.

It is important to note that self-hypnosis is not designed to be used instead of drug therapy. Rather, as previously stated, it is appropriate in conjunction with inhalers prescribed by your doctor. In time the need for inhalers may become less or indeed your doctor may decide you no longer require medication.


## High Blood Pressure

High blood pressure is very prevalent in Western society. Approximately 15 per cent of the population can be regarded as hypertensive. Hypertension can be classified into primary (essential) hypertension and secondary hypertension. Primary hypertension accounts for 85 per cent of those with elevated blood pressure, while secondary hypertension is responsible for the remaining 15 per cent of high blood pressure cases. Secondary hypertension means that the elevated blood pressure is due to an identifiable cause such as kidney disease or the use of oral contraceptive drugs.

The British Hypertensive Society use the arbitrary figures of 160mm Hg systolic and 90mm Hg diastolic as guidance for the treatment of blood pressure. In order for your doctor to diagnose high blood pressure, it is necessary to obtain a reading that represents your usual blood pressure. This requires that an average of several blood pressure readings be taken. If hypertension is diagnosed it is important that 'secondary causes' are ruled out. Your doctor will automatically check this for you.

You may ask why it is so vital that high blood pressure be treated. If blood pressure is even slightly or moderately elevated above normal pressure readings and remains unchecked over a number of years, the condition can damage target organs such as the brain, heart, kidneys and eyes. Blood pressure at an unusually high level represents a medical emergency as it may cause 'weakened' arteries to rupture, and if they happen to be in the brain the person may have a stroke or even die.

If your doctor records a slightly elevated blood pressure reading, you should be monitored closely over the succeeding few months and commence 'non-drug' management immediately. This will include controlling stress and anxiety, stopping smoking and losing some weight (if appropriate), regular exercise, and a reduction in salt, caffeine and alcohol intake. Not only can self-hypnosis on a daily basis help with these areas of 'non-drug' management (see relevant sections in this chapter dealing with anxiety, smoking and slimming), but it can also be used to actively alter the tone in your blood vessels and so directly reduce your blood pressure (see chapter 3). The following exercise

utilizes imagery and suggestions stemming from an understanding of the physical mechanisms involved in controlling
blood pressure.

## Exercise

1 Close your eyes and allow yourself to enter a peaceful
  hypnotic state.
2 Visualize your heart as a muscular bag in the centre of
  your chest, pumping blood into the arteries and all around
  your body. You may wish to see these arteries as muscular
  tubes, expanding as the blood pumps into them and then
  slowly contracting down once more.
3 Imagine the messages coming from your brain, down
  through your spinal cord and out via the nerves (known as
  the 'sympathetic nerves') to your heart and blood vessels.
  Colour code these messages: red when there are a lot of
  messages passing to the heart and blue when there is a
  reduction in the number of messages.
4 Notice the effect of the 'red' messages. The heart pumps
  rapidly and forcefully and the arteries squeeze down
  tightly. A rise in the blood pressure results from the
  combined effect.
5 In contrast, notice the effect of the 'blue' messages. Your
  heart rate slows down and pumps with more ease. The
  blood vessels dilate and relax.
6 Focus on visualizing the effect of these 'blue' messages
  until you become aware of your body feeling deeply
  relaxed.
7 Reinforce this feeling of relaxation using imagery and
  suggestions of your own choosing before bringing this
  exercise to an end.

## Irritable Bowel Syndrome

This condition involves the experience of pain or discomfort in the abdomen associated with constipation or

looseness of bowel motion. As it appears to be a stress-related disorder (Zisook and DePaul, 1977), approaches which can help you to become a more relaxed person (such as those included in chapter 3) are once again relevant here. Your work may also involve addressing possible underlying problems and secondary gains (see chapter 4).

The value of hypnotherapy with irritable bowel syndrome has been impressively documented (see, for instance, Whorwell et al, 1987). The following exercise involves working directly on symptoms of an overactive bowel. It focuses on the pathways and mechanism by which the subconscious mind influences the gut. Although the control of the bowel is more complicated than this exercise suggests, the work to follow serves as a simple means by which you can use imagery in self-hypnosis to influence its activity.

## Exercise

1 Close your eyes and allow yourself to enter a peaceful self-hypnotic state.
2 Imagine your bowel being similar in appearance to corrugated tubing. See it move – a slow movement like a wave down a caterpillar's body.
3 This wave of activity is under the control of two types of nerves, much like telephone lines.
4 One of these 'telephone pathways' is known as the 'parasympathetic nerve'. When activated it passes messages to the bowel to increase activity and to open. See this 'telephone line' in your mind, running from the base of your brain to your bowel, and identify it with the colour red.
5 The other 'telephone pathway' is known as the 'sympathetic nerve'. It operates in a reverse way, telling the bowel to decrease activity and to close. You can visualize this 'telephone line' starting in your spinal cord (about half-way down your back) and colour it blue.
6 Now imagine the messages going down both lines to the bowel as pulses. Allow the pulse rate in the 'blue line'

to speed up, while you decrease the pulse rate in the 'red line'.

7 As the number of pulses increases in the 'blue line' and decreases in the 'red line' see the activity in your bowel decreasing.

8 This exercise becomes complete as you imagine your bowel becoming calm, relaxed and rested, able to function in a normal, healthy and comfortable manner once more.


## Cancer

As an adjunct to more standard approaches of treatment, self-hypnosis can be very useful to the cancer patient. Self-suggestion and imagery can be utilized, both in and out of hypnosis, to control pain (see relevant section in this chapter). Practising self-hypnosis during a session of chemotherapy may help time to pass more quickly and allow stress levels to be reduced. It can also help to minimize the distressing side-effects of such treatment, including nausea, vomiting, tiredness and loss of appetite. For example, Rosenberg (1983) suggests the following can be adapted to help nausea and stimulation of the appetite: '. . . imagery of a cool, comfortable fog or light rain touching the cheeks, being breathed in and pleasantly numbing the tongue, mouth, throat, stomach etc'. Experiment and use what works best for you. Self-hypnosis and the knowledge that there is something you can do to help yourself can greatly improve morale and counteract feelings of helplessness.

Exciting research carried out in the past decade (Hall et al, 1984) has shown that relaxation techniques and self-hypnosis can be used to increase defence mechanisms and thus strengthen the body's immunity system. The following exercise uses imagery as suggested by the Simontons (1978) to enhance the body's immune processes. Be creative, inventing your own personal imagery if it feels more appropriate.

*Exercise*

1 Close your eyes and allow yourself to enter a peaceful self-hypnotic state.
2 Visualize your white blood cells (the body's natural 'killer cells') as a strong and powerful army of warriors.
3 Imagine the cancer cells, perhaps already partially beaten down by radiotherapy or chemotherapy, as weak animals such as snails or slugs.
4 See in your mind the army of warriors win an easy battle against these weak animals.
5 Visualize the dead cancer cells being flushed out of the body.
6 Imagine your body healthy and strong, free from cancer. Enjoy and become fully absorbed in that process before bringing this exercise to an end.

Whether you wish to improve the quality of your life in general or work on a specific problem, to achieve the full benefit from your self-hypnosis it may, as we have already mentioned, be necessary to experiment with various techniques, suggestions and imagery to find out what will work best for you. This process will require time, repetition and patience. As suggested in chapter 4, if you have been working on yourself for some time, but are still no nearer to achieving your goals, it may be that you will benefit from the guidance of a trained therapist who can help your progress down that road to success.

# 7

# Taking It Further

The chief phenomena [of hypnosis] are indisputable . . . I
implore you carefully investigate this important subject.

John Elliotson

## FINDING A PRACTITIONER

THROUGH THE COURSE OF LEARNING self-hypnosis it may
be that you wish to see a practitioner for some extra
instruction or receive help with an area which you feel is
too much to take on by yourself. Whatever your reason for
wishing to visit a therapist, it is important that you find
someone who is both genuine and professional.

Unfortunately, the law at present, in Britain at least,
makes it possible for anyone to practise as a hypnotherapist.
Also, due to the fact that the length and quality of training
can vary considerably, it is worth checking out certain
points with prospective therapists. These should include:

- How long was their training and what qualifications do
  they hold?
- Are they registered, and if so with which organization?
- How long have they been practising?
- What is their policy on payment for sessions? (I would feel
  uneasy about a therapist who, prior to treatment, charges
  for a set number of sessions in advance. Generally, it is
  not possible at the outset to gauge accurately how many
  sessions will be required.)
- If you are seeking help with a specific problem, do they

89

have experience of working with this area? (Just because someone is trained in hypnosis does not necessarily mean he or she is going to be competent at treating all areas.)

In addition to ensuring that you feel confident about the therapist's professional background, it is also important to treatment that you like and feel comfortable with this person. The organizations listed in the Useful Addresses section on page 97 will be able to provide you with the details of qualified practitioners in your area.


## CONCLUSION

> We are not in a position in which we have nothing to work with. We already have a start; we already have capacities, talents, direction, missions, callings.
>
> The job is, if we are willing to take it seriously, to help ourselves to be more perfectly what we are, to be more full, more actualising, more realising, in fact, what we are in potentiality.
>
> Abraham Maslow

This introduction to self-hypnosis brings together the most practical and useful techniques and concepts that I have come across in my personal and professional study of the subject. I trust you have enjoyed it, found it useful and feel stimulated to learn more. If you have gained benefit from even one idea outlined in this book, then I will feel that my effort has been justified.

Most of us throughout our lives fulfil a mere fraction of our true natural potential. It is my hope that this publication will go some way towards showing you how powerful you really can be. Taking responsibility for contributing to your mental and physical well-being can be an empowering experience, helping you to feel more in control in all areas of life. Learning to redirect your internal natural talents to your advantage can help you to improve the quality of your health and life. My best wishes are with you in this work. Treat yourself better!

# References

Andreas, C and Andreas, S, *Heart of the Mind, Engaging Your Inner Power to Change with Neuro-linguistic Programming*, Real People Press, 1989

Araoz, D L, 'Human Sexuality, Hypnosis and Therapy', in *Developing Ericksonian Therapy* (eds J Zeig and S Lankton), Brunner-Mazel, 1988

Bandler, R, *Using Your Brain For A Change*, Real People Press, 1985

Bishay, E G and Lee, C, 'Studies of the effects of hypnoanesthesia on regional blood flow by transcutaneous oxygen monitoring', *American Journal of Clinical Hypnosis*, Vol 27(1), pp 64–9, 1984

Bresler, D E, 'Meeting an Inner Adviser', in *Handbook of Hypnotic Suggestions and Metaphors, An American Society of Clinical Hypnosis Book* (ed D C Hammond), W W Norton & Co, New York and London, 1990

Caddy, E, *Footprints On The Path*, Findhorn Press, Scotland, 1971

Chapman, L, Goodell, H and Woolf, H, 'Changes in tissue vulnerability induced during hypnotic suggestion', *Journal of Psychosomatic Research*, Vol 4, pp 99–105, 1959

D'Eston, C, *Observations sur le magnetisme animal*, P Fr Didot, Paris, Lejeune, 1780

Domangue, B, Margolis, C, Lieberman, D and Kaji, H, 'Biochemical correlates of hypnoanalgesia in arthritic pain patients', *Journal of Clinical Psychiatry*, Vol 46(6), pp 235–8, 1985

Elliotson, J, *Harveian Oration*, Walton and Mitchell, London, 1846

Ewin, D M, 'Hypnosis in burn therapy', in *Hypnosis* (eds G D Burrows, D R Colison and L Dennerstein), Elsevier/North Holland Press, Amsterdam and New York, 1979

French, T M and Alexander, F, 'Psychogenic factors in bronchial asthma', *Journal of Psychosomatic Medicine*, Vol 4, 1941

Gargiulo, T, 'Influence of training in hypnotic responsivity on hypnotically suggested analgesia', unpublished doctoral dissertation, California Coast University, 1983

Gibbons, D E, *Applied Hypnosis and Hyperempiria*, Plenum, New York, 1979

Godefroy, C H, *Super Health, How to Control Your Body's Natural Defences*, Piatkus Books, 1992

Goethe, J Wolfgang von, *Faust, A Tragedy*, translated in the original meters by Bayard Taylor, Random House (Modern Library), New York, 1967

Hall, H R, Longo, S and Dixon, R H, 'Hypnosis and the immune system: The effect of hypnosis on T and B cell function', in *Imagination and Healing* (ed A A Sheikh), Baywood Publishing Co, New York, 1984

Hammond, D C, 'The Master Control Room Technique' and 'Reducing Dermatologic Irritation', in *Handbook of Hypnotic Suggestions and Metaphors, An American Society of Clinical Hypnosis Book* (ed D C Hammond), W W Norton & Co, New York and London, 1990

Hay, L L, *The Power is Within You*, Eden Grove Editions, London, 1991

Hearne, K, 'Harping on the evils of tobacco fails to convince smokers', *European Journal of Clinical Hypnosis*, Edition No 3, April 1994

Hull, C L, *Hypnosis and Suggestibility: An Experimental Approach*, Appleton-Century-Crofts, New York, 1933

Jacobson, E, *Progressive Relaxation*, University of Chicago Press, 1938, 1974

Kaji, H, Domange, B, Fink, G et al, 'Effects of hypnoanalgesia on levels of Beta-Endorphin-like components', Eighth International Congress of Pharmacology, Tokyo, 1981

Kaplan, H S, *Disorders of Sexual Desire*, Brunner-Mazel, New York, 1979

Lipiccolo, J and Hogan, D R, 'Sexual Dysfunction', in *Behavioural Medicine: Theory and Practice* (eds O F Pomerleau and J P Brady), Williams & Wilkins, Baltimore and London, 1979

# References

Maslow, A H, *The Farther Reaches of Human Nature*, Viking Press Inc, New York, 1971

McGlashen, T, Evans, F and Orne, M, 'The nature of hypnotic analgesia and placebo responses to experimental pain', *Psychosomatic Medicine*, Vol 31, pp 227–46, 1969

Norwood, R, *Women Who Love Too Much*, N Y Pocket Books, 1985

Orne, M, 'Mechanisms of hypnotic pain control', in *Advances in Pain Research and Therapy*, Vol 1 (eds J Bonica and A Albe-Fessard), Lippincott, New York, 1976

Prather, D C, 'Promoted Mental Practice as a Flight Simulator', *Journal of Applied Psychology*, Vol 57, pp 353–5, 1973

Rausch, V, 'Cholecystectomy with self-hypnosis', *American Journal of Clinical Hypnosis*, Vol 22, January 1980

Rosenberg, S W, 'Hypnosis in cancer care: Imagery to enhance the control of the physiological and psychological "side-effects" of cancer therapy', *American Journal of Clinical Hypnosis*, Vol 25 (2–3), pp 122–7, 1983

Rossi, E L and Cheek, D B, *Mind-Body Therapy, Methods of Ideodynamic Healing in Hypnosis*, W W Norton & Co, New York and London, 1988

Schuller, R H, *Tough Times Never Last, But Tough People Do!*, Thomas Nelson Inc, Bantam Books Edition, Nashville, 1984

Simonton, O C, Matthews-Simonton, S and Creighton, J L, *Getting well again: a step-by-step, self-help guide to overcoming cancer for patients and their families*, Bantam Books, New York, 1978

Stanton, H E, 'Visualization for treating insomnia', in *Handbook of Hypnotic Suggestions and Metaphors*, An American Society of Clinical Hypnosis Book (ed D C Hammond), W W Norton & Co, New York and London, 1990

Stein, C, 'The clenched fist technique as a hypnotic procedure in clinical psychotherapy', *American Journal of Clinical Hypnosis*, Vol 6, pp 113–19, 1963

Walch, S L, 'The red balloon technique of hypnotherapy: A clinical note', *International Journal of Clinical and Experimental Hypnosis*, Vol 24(1), pp 10–12, 1976

Whorwell, P J, Prior, A and Clogan, S M, 'Hypnotherapy in severe irritable bowel syndrome: Further experience', *Gut*, Vol 28(4), pp 423–5, 1987

Zisook, S and DePaul, R A, 'Emotional factors in inflammatory bowel disease', *Southern Medical Journal*, Vol 70, pp 716–19, 1977

# Further Reading

Andreas, S and Andreas C, *Change Your Mind And Keep The Change*, Real People Press, 1987

Bandler, R and Grinder, J, *Frogs into Princes*, Real People Press, 1979

Bandler, R and Grinder, J, *Trance-formations, Neurolinguistic Programming and the Structure of Hypnosis*, Real People Press, 1981

Bandler, R, *Using Your Brain For A Change*, Real People Press, 1985

Gawain, S, *Creative Visualization*, Bantam Books, 1978

Hay, L L, *The Power is Within You*, Eden Grove Editions, 1991

Peiffer, V, *Positive Thinking*, Element Books, 1989

# Useful Addresses

If you wish to learn more about hypnosis and hypnotherapy and would like information on possible courses, seminars and workshops being held in your area, please apply to the workshops listed below. (The addresses are provided for information purposes only and are not necessarily a source of recommendation).

**Asia**
Indian Society for
Clinical and
Experimental
Hypnosis (ISCEH)
Secretary: Dr H Jana
40/301 Saraswatinagar
Near Azad Society
Ahmedabad – 380015,
Gujarat, India

Japanese Society of
Hypnosis (JSH)
Secretary: Dr Noboru
Takaishi
C/o Harano Laboratory
Graduate School of
Education Center
University of Tsukub

3–29–1 Ohtsuka,
Bunkyo-Ku
Tokyo 112, Japan

**Australia**
Australian Society of
Hypnosis (ASH)
Secretary: Dr Mark Earl
Austin Hospital
Heidelberg, Victoria 3084

**Canada**
Canadian Society of
Hypnosis (CSH)
(Alberta Division)
Secretary: Ms Glenda
Labelle
7027 Edgemont Drive
Calgary, Alberta, T3A 2H9

Ontario Society of Clinical
Hypnosis (OSCH)
Secretary: Ms Patricia
Derraugh
200 St Clair Ave W
Suite 402
Toronto, Ontario,
M4V 1R1

**Europe and Middle East**
Osterreichische Gesellschaft
für Autogenes Training und
Allgemeine Psychotherapie
(OGATAP)
Secretary: Dr Erik Bolcs
Testarellogasse 31/13
A-1130 Vienna
Austria

Vlaamse Vereniging voor
Autogene Training en
Hypnotherapy v.z.w.
(VATHYP)
Secretary: Dr Pieter Roosen
Gebroeders Verhaegenstr 13
2800 Mechelen
Belgium

Tieteellinen Hypnoosi
– Vetenskaplig Hypnos
(TH-VH)
Secretary: Dr Maija
Kaariainen
Kanervakuja 2 as 4
21380 Aura
Finland

Deutsche Gesellschaft für
artzliche Hypnose und
Autogenes Training e.V.
(DGAHAT)
Secretary: Frau Elke Koch
Oberforstbacher Strasse 416
D-5100 Aachen
Germany

German Society of
Hypnosis (GSH)
Secretary: Ms Helga
Husken-Janssen
Druffelsweg 3
Coesfeld g-4420
Germany

Milton Erickson Gesellschaft
für Klinische Hypnose e. V.
(MEG)
Secretary: Dr Wilhelm Gerl
Konradstrasse 16
DW-8000 Munchen 40
Germany

Deutsche Gessellschaft
für Klinische und
Experimentelle Hypnose
(DGKEH)
Secretary: Dr Uwe
Gabert-Varga
Gerokstrasse 65
7000 Stuttgart 1
Germany

Irish Society of Clinical
and Experimental Hypnosis
(IR-SCEH)
Secretary: Mr P G Gamble
59 McCurtain Street
Cork
Ireland

Israel Society for Clinical
and
Experimental Hypnosis
(IS-SCEH)
Secretary: Prof Karl Fuchs
44 Hanassi Avenue
Haifa 34643
Israel

Associazionne Medica
Italiana per
lo Studio dell Ipnosi (AMISI)
Secretary: Dr G Mosconi
Via Paisiello 28
20131 Milano, MI
Italy

Centro Studi de Ipnosi
Clinica E Psiocoterapie 'H
Bernheim' (CSICPHB)
Secretary: Dr G Guantieri
Via Valverde 65
Verona 37122
Italy

Nederlandse Vereniging voor
Hypnotherapie (NVVH)
Secretary: Dr Chr Koopmans
PO Box 4085
3502 HB Utrecht
Netherlands

Norwegian Society of
Clinical and Experimental
Hypnosis (NSCEH)
Secretary: Dr Gunnar Rosen
The Pain Clinic
Bergen University Hospital
N-5021 Bergen
Norway

Swedish Society for Clinical
and Experimental Hypnosis
(SSCEH)
Secretary: Dr Torbjorn
Hellenius
P O Box 104
s-69322, Degerfors
Sweden

Swiss Medical Society of
Hypnosis (SMSH)
Secretary: Dr Patrick Noyer
Av Leopold-Robert 73A
2300 La Chaux-de-Fonds
Switzerland

British Hypnosis Research
(BHR)
Director: Mr Stephen
Brooks
St Matthews House
1 Brick Row
Darley Abbey
Derby DE22 1DQ
UK

British Society of
Experimental and Clinical
Hypnosis (BSECH)
Secretary: Ms Phyllis Alden
The Department of
Psychology
Grimsby General Hospital
Scartho Road
Grimsby DN33 2BA
UK

British Society of Medical
and
Dental Hypnosis (BSMDH)
Secretary: Ms Rhona
Jackson
17 Keppel View Road
Kimberworth
Rotherham
UK

The Hypnotherapy
Register, held by The
National Council Of
Psychotherapists (NCP)
Secretary: Mr W R Broom
24 Rickmansworth Road
Watford
Hertfordshire WD1 7HT
UK

Scottish Branch – British
Society of Medical and
Dental Hypnosis (SB-BSMDH)
Secretary: Dr Prem C Misra
C/o Parkhead Hospital
Salamanca Street
Glasgow G31 5ES
UK

**South Africa**
South African Society of
Clinical Hypnosis (SASCH)
Secretary: Dr Pieter W Nel
29 Isabel Street
Kilner Park XI, 0186

**South America**
Sociedade Brasileira de
Hipnose (SBH)
Secretary: Dr Joao Jorge C
Nogueira
Avenida Mem de Sa. 197
Rio de Janeiro
Brazil

**USA**
American Society of
Clinical Hypnosis (ASCH)
Secretary: Mr William
Hoffman Jr
Suite 291
2200 East Devon Avenue
Des Plaines, IL,
600118–4534

Society For Clinical and
Experimental Hypnosis
(SCEH)
Secretary: Mrs Eloise
Bredder
6728 Old McLean
Village Road
McLean, VA, 22101

# Index

agoraphobia 64–5
amnesia 6
anaesthesia 14, 37
anxiety, *see* phobia
anxiolytic drugs 20, 63–4
arthritis 26
asthma 26

benzodiazepines 20, 63–4
Bernheim, Hyppolyte-Marie 15
blood pressure, high, *see*
    hypertension
Braid, James 14–15
British Medical Association 16–17

caffeine, effects of 20
cancer 87–8
Charcot, Jean Martin 15–16
chemotherapy, reducing side-
    effects of 87
commitment 34
confidence, lack of 66–8
conscious mind 4, 37
control 7–8, 9, 10

diary, keeping a 35
dieting 59–60
distractions, dealing with
    41–2
driving test 25–6

eczema 79–80
Einstein, Albert 24
electroencephalograph (EEG) 6
Elliotson, John 14
epilepsy 38
Esdaile, James 14
Eslon, Charles d' 13
expectations, unrealistic 30
eye fixation technique 46–7, 50

fear, *see* phobia
First World War 17
'fist' technique 67–8
Freud, Sigmund 16, 17

goals, clarification of 33–4
Goethe, Johann Wolfgang 35

habit disorders 53–63
Hull, Clark L 17
hypertension 27, 83–5
hypnosis: definition of 3–4
    myths about 5–10
    as entertainment 9–10
    to anaesthetize 14
    mechanism of 19
    where to practise 38–9
    time to practise 39–41
    precautions when using 38
hypnotic inductions 46–51
hypnotic subjects 8–9, 29–30

imaginal rehearsal 25
imagination, power of 24–7
inner adviser 32
insomnia 75–7
irritable bowel syndrome 85–7

Liébeault, Ambrose-August 15

magnetism 12, 13, 15
mental overactivity 41–2
Mesmer, Franz Anton 12–13
migraine 26–7
mind/body relationship 19–21, 27
motivation 31

Nancy School of Hypnosis 15
negative thinking 22–3, 26, 66

pain: types of 70
  control 71–4
phobia 63–6
positive thinking 22–4, 66, 72
post-hypnotic suggestion 24, 39
  see also suggestion
premenstrual syndrome (PMS) 77–9
psychoanalysis 16
Puységur, Marquis Armand
  de 13–14

Raush, Victor 37
relaxation, exercises in 44–5,
  47–8, 50

secondary gains 31–3
senses, utilization of 43–4
sexual problems 68–70
sleep 6, 13, 14
slimming 58–63
  see also weight loss
smoking 31–2, 53–8
stage hypnotists 9–10, 17
staircase induction 48–51
'stop' technique 22, 61
subconscious mind 4
suggestion 15, 21–4, 42–3
support, importance of 34–5
'swish' technique 55–8

trance 4–5

weight loss 31
  see also slimming

Zoist, The 14